Multi-Million Dollar Dollar Dental Practice

How to <u>Net</u> $1 Million A Year In Your Dental Practice... Even In A Recession

Dr. Mike Kesner

Table of Contents

Acknowledgements

To Debbie: You are the love of my life. Thank you for a wonderful 31 years of marriage. I look forward to the next 31 years. The success we now enjoy would not have happened without your unconditional support and encouragement over the years. You are a very special woman.

To Carey: You are a wonderful son who I am truly blessed to have. I am proud of the great husband you are to Ashley and the loving father you are to Caden and Micah. You will continue to be successful in everything that you have decided to undertake and will decide in the future.

To Heather: You are a wonderful daughter who I am truly blessed to have. I am proud of the wonderful wife you are to John. You are a beautiful, smart and compassionate lady. You are a great mother to Ethan. Thank you for the hard work you put into making our dental practice a success.

To My Team: The success of our practice could not have happened without you and your hard work.

You do so much to make my life a lot easier. Thank you for your commitment to build a dental practice that stands out in the crowd.

To Greg and Logan: Thank you for your passion and commitment to help dentists become successful and fulfilled in their practices. Your hard work in the profession has made and continues to make a difference in the lives of many doctors and their families.

Introduction

From Burn-Out To Millionaire

I have been practicing General Dentistry since 1984. When I graduated from dental school I immediately took out a loan and opened my practice as a new start-up. After 3 years, since I had out-grown my 1200 square foot lease space, I built out a larger 1600 square foot lease space, about a mile down the road.

My practice philosophy, at that time, was to see as many patients as possible which I brought in with advertising. I was seeing 60-80 new patients a month but, since I didn't know how to get patients to say "yes" to the treatment they needed, I was real busy but my practice was not very profitable. I also did not have any systems in place, so most of the time I felt as if I had a tiger by-the-tail. My practice was in control of me instead of me being in control of my practice.

This began my search for a better way of doing dentistry, so I began seeking out the various gurus and consultants in dentistry. Since I thought that the busyness of my practice was the problem, I sought out consultants with the philosophy in dentistry that promotes low patient flow and high-end dentistry. This philosophy focuses on seeing very few patients a day, but doing only "the best and finest" dentistry. This translates into focusing on doing high fee/big case dentistry.

I took many continuing educational programs in TMJ, occlusion, orthopedics and orthodontics and full mouth re-construction, along with practice management seminars and in-office consultants.

After four years in this new office, and still not being very successful with my chosen mode of practice, I decided that the reason, for my lack of success, was that I was in the wrong area of town. I decided to sell my practice and start all over again in a more affluent area of town. I believed this would be more in line with my practice philosophy.

In this new area of town, I built out a 2250 square foot lease space in a professional building. I started my practice over again from scratch, but this time only trying to attract patients that were interested in comprehensive dental care.

My new patient exams were 90 minutes with the doctor, complete with mounted models, x-rays and intra-oral and extra-oral photographs. This was followed by a separate 30 minute treatment conference, a week later. Following this appointment, the patient was then scheduled with the hygienist. On top of all of this, I did not accept any insurance assignments and did not offer any financing options to patients. A patient had to be pretty committed to make it through this whole process, and, as you can imagine, many were not.

I was not anymore successful in this new, more affluent area of town, with my "high-end" type of practice philosophy. I spent thousands of dollars on practice consultants and gurus that I hoped could show me the way to this "best-dentist-in-town" type of practice. I had visions of patients flocking to me from different states and countries for all their full mouth re-constructions and high-end cosmetics and difficult TMJ cases.

After 13 years of trying to build this type of practice, I was stuck at a gross production of only $500,000 per year, which meant that I was netting only around $120,000 per year. This was far too much work and far too much risk for only $120K per year. I desperately wanted success, but the harder I tried, the harder success was to find.

Little did I know that, my lack of success problem wasn't the area of town my practice was located in.

**The problem was that the practice
model, I was desperately trying to
implement, did not work for me.**

I have seen a few dentists make this type of
practice model work, but I couldn't.

I always wanted to have a practice that grossed $1
million a year, but no matter how hard I tried or how
many consultants I hired, I just could not make it
happen. After several years of trying and failing at
different philosophies and models of practicing
dentistry, I decided to give up. Dentistry was just
too hard to be taking home only $120,000 a year
before taxes.

**In 1997 I got burned out on
dentistry and I decided to try
to find a way to get out.**

My wife, who is a surgical nurse, and I had
worked with and helped to start a missionary
medical and dental ministry in Guatemala. I was
devoting a lot of my time and energy there. We
were helping to build a clinic in a remote village in
the mountains of Guatemala. We had been taking
medical and dental teams from the U.S. for years, to
this remote clinic.

Dentistry for me had just become a way to finance my
missionary endeavors. I had given up on my dream

of success in dentistry. Now, I just wanted to make as much money as possible so I could afford to get out of dentistry, as soon as possible.

In 1997 I decided to sell my practice so I hired a practice broker and put it on the market.

I realized that I could make just as much, or even more money, in dentistry, working as an associate and not have to put up with the headaches and the risk associated with running a business. My plan was to sell my practice and become an associate for that buyer .

It was a very scary decision for me, but I was so disillusioned with my inability to be successful in dentistry that I decided to go ahead and list my practice. Two years later, in 1999, I found a buyer. He was an orthodontist who was buying dental practices as investments. In September 1999 I sold my practice to him. I stayed on and worked for him as an associate in my office, and I also worked in three other practices that he owned. During the three years that I worked as an associate, I tripled my income doing lots of dentistry in these three practices.

This all changed quite suddenly one night. The orthodontist's wife, who is a general dentist, caught him at a hotel with another woman.

When he walked outside of the hotel, she ran over him three times in the parking lot with her Mercedes Benz - killing him.

For months, this event made international news. A made-for-TV movie was produced on this story. The wife was interviewed from prison by Oprah a few times and there were at least two books written about the whole incident.

Now, I found myself back in a position of being able to own my practice again. For two years, I was in a process of purchasing my practice back from the estate of the now deceased orthodontist.

After buying my practice back in 2004, I decided that this time I was going to do whatever it took to become wealthy and successful in dentistry. I had spent the last 19 years in dentistry trying to become successful, but I had never really come to the place in my life where I made a commitment to do whatever it took to achieve success.

I was now willing to do <u>whatever was necessary,</u> that was ethical, honest and legal, in order to build

a multi-million- dollar practice.

I had said and determined many times before, that I wanted success, but I had a list of things I was not willing to do to achieve it. What I was really saying was that I did not want a multi-million-dollar per year practice bad enough to do what was necessary to make it happen. What I really wanted was to do things my way, regardless of whether patients wanted it or not.

> **You have to make the decision that you are willing to do whatever it takes to be successful and get rid of the list of things that you won't do or that you believe are beneath your practice philosophy.**

I also found out that, to be successful you have to be willing to take a close look at yourself. The reason you are not successful is you. I got myself into this place, so I knew I had to change the things in me that hindered my success, in order to go to a new place. What got me where I was would not get me where I wanted to be.

In this day and age, your practice has to be consumer friendly in order to excel. People want convenience and service and they want it now. A successful dental practice is one that meets the needs and wants of patients.

Working for three years as an associate for the orthodontist helped me to get over my high fee, large case and low patient number philosophy of practicing dentistry that I couldn't make work.

I began to study everything I could get my hands on in the area of success in business and success in life. I went to all kinds of seminars. I hired consultants and coaches both in the dental field and out of the dental field. I got personal counseling to weed out false beliefs, thought patterns and behaviors that hindered my success. I tried all kinds of different techniques, systems and marketing. I tweaked what worked and threw out what didn't.

Over the next six years, after I made this commitment to "do whatever it takes", I experienced a quantum leap growth going from $675,000 a year in gross collections to $4.2 million in gross collections! This growth has allowed me to net over $1 million per year.

I had finally discovered the necessary keys to success in dentistry. I had learned and figured out the systems, techniques, procedures, marketing techniques, behavioral techniques, and practice philosophies that work to build a multi-million dollar dental practice.

I had discovered how to build a practice that is <u>recession proof</u> and will continue to grow and thrive even in a down economy.

I did all of this in a town that has at least two dentists on every corner!

Dentistry is great. It is one of the few professions where you are in control of your income. You can practice however you want; you can do the procedures you want; and you can become as successful as you want. There are not many other professions that allow that kind of control over your destiny.

There are strategies and systems that I use to help dentists implement in their practices, which give them a $10,000 increase in their personal monthly before-tax income, after a few months. What other professions are out there that can give you that level of control over your income? - where you can give yourself a $10K per month raise - Dentistry is great!

Unfortunately, most dentists don't enjoy that level of success. They want that level of success, but they don't know how to get it.

I understand... I was at that place for 19 years. It is a frustrating place to be!

One of the things I have learned is that <u>you cannot do this on your own.</u> You have to have coaches, consultants and mentors who know what they are doing and know how to help you attain this level of success.

You also have to have a great team of employees that are committed and have an incentive to help you attain this level of success. I have found that the dentists, who try to do this on their own, never make it happen. If you could do this on your own, you would already be enormously successful.

I am a wet-fingered practicing dentist that knows the way to a multi-million-dollar practice because I have done it and I continue to do it on a daily basis. I decided to write this book, to help other dentists see and understand that they can develop a multimillion-dollar practice too.

You too, can net $1 million a year or more! If I am doing it, then you can too.

In reading this book, I want to open your mind to the possibility that, if this is something you want, then you too can attain it.

You must have help.
You cannot do it on your own.

You cannot attain this level of success by just reading this book. There are things about yourself, about your team, and about your practice, that are holding you back from the level of success you want. You cannot see these road blocks or change them without help from someone that has been there and knows the way.

There are some good dental coaches and consultants in dentistry that can help you; Some are dentists, and some are not.

The important thing to realize is
that you cannot go to a new place
if you don't know the way there.

You need help from somebody that knows the way, has been there before, and more importantly, knows how to take you there. Whatever got you to where you are now will not get you to where you want to be. You can only get to that next place with outside help.

Some consultants in the dental industry have some good ideas, but sometimes they are just that... good ideas. Many of the things, that consultants told me during my 19 years of frustration in dentistry, were good ideas that worked in theory, but in reality did not work for me.

You can't afford to do something that is a good theoretical idea but is not something you can replicate in your practice. This is what I did for the first 19 years of my career.

High fee, high case average and low patient flow practices are good ideas that, in my opinion, very few dentists are able to pull off. I didn't and still don't have what it takes to make that kind of practice work, and, in my experience, most other dentists don't either. There are very few of these types of practices around that are successful.

In this low, new patient flow type of practice, the case average has to be very high in order to be financially successful. The number of patients who need large amounts of dentistry done, and have the ability and desire to pay that much on their mouths, is a small slice of the dental market. There are not too many dentists that can pull this one off but, in theory, it is possible because there are some dentists doing it.

Most of these high fee, large case or cosmetic only boutique types of practices have experienced a 30+ percent drop in their revenue in this down economy over the last two years.

Not too long ago, I read some writings from a dental consultant who is not a dentist. He said that it was good that one of his clients only saw four new patients a month. His reasoning was that most new patients were just rejects, from other practices, that waste your time and don't do the dentistry you diagnose. Wow! That has not been my experience.

My experience is that if the patients are not doing the dental treatment I diagnose, it is usually because I and/or my team are not doing a good enough job making it easy for patients to say "yes" to what they need.

This kind of low, new patient volume and high case average philosophy might work in the hands of a few dentists, but it didn't work in mine. I would hate to try to make this kind of practice work in our present economy. If I only had four, new patients a month, I would be majorly stressed out! I much prefer my present new patient count of 150 per month.

The more new patients I have, the more relaxed I am and the less pressure I feel to "have to sell this case". I typically see around 10 new patients a day so if Mr. Smith says..."I don't care if my teeth are decayed, cracked and broken. They have been that way for 40 years."...I don't feel the need to lean on him and tell him in a nice way that he is an idiot. I know that I have 9 more new patients that day, so I can just say... "That's OK. I'll be here when you get a toothache."

You all have had patients like this. They don't have a very high value on their health. Maybe that value will change when they get a bad toothache, and maybe it won't. I don't believe that anything you say will make people value something that they never have valued before. You are just beating your head against a wall.

If Mr. Smith was the last one of my "four new patients" for that month, and I knew that my bills had not been paid yet, I am sure that my attitude with him would be a little different.

I don't like having that feeling inside which tells me... "You really need this case". That doesn't serve me or the patient very well.

At my present level of monthly production, four new patients a month would mean that they would have to do around $75,000 in dentistry each! There are not too many patients out there with mouths that bombed out. I just prefer to work on all those 150 "rejects" from other practices every month.

In November 2007 I built a new office which is 6000 square feet and has 17 treatment rooms. We had reached the point where my old office of 2250 square feet and 6 treatment rooms were limiting my capacity to do the dentistry we were capable of doing. I realized that I could not grow the practice any bigger in my present facility. Our production immediately went up 15% just by increasing the capacity in our new facility.

I found that, as I grew my practice larger and larger, the consultants out there, who were capable of consulting at this level, were pretty much nonexistent. I was <u>netting</u> $1 million per year and most consultants are just trying to get dentists to <u>gross</u> $1 million per year. I realized that there was a need to have a consulting program to help doctors grow multi-million-dollar practices and really get wealthy in dentistry.

I began a coaching/consulting company called Quantum Leap Success in Dentistry for the purpose of taking dentists to that next level in practice success. I teach my clients what I am doing that works to make a multi-million-dollar practice. My systems, techniques and strategies are not theory or just good ideas. These are things that work day-in and day-out to net me over $1 million dollars a year.

Our niche is giving doctors the tools to make this kind of Quantum Leap growth in their practices

If what I talk about in this book fits who you are and where you want to go with your career, then take advantage of the *free one-hour phone consultation with one of our practice consultants* on page 161. The consultant will be able to talk with you about your specific situation and see if we are a fit for you.

The main thing to realize is that you cannot build a multi-million-dollar practice on your own. If you could, you already would have. The money you spend on a good consultant may seem like a lot, but it is a bargain, when you build the practice of your dreams that changes your life forever.

Quantum Leap Success in Dentistry is a "high octane" coaching and consulting company for dentists who are serious about building the practice of their dreams. This is for dentists who are at the point in their lives where they are willing to make the commitment to make the changes, in themselves and their practices, necessary for huge success.

Quantum Leap is not for those who are going to be satisfied with small increments of growth in their practice. We focus on starting and maintaining Quantum Leap growth. I have found that you need to know how to start the momentum of a rapidly growing practice, and then keep that momentum going.

Like the momentum in a football game, it is easier to keep the momentum going when you already have it than to regain the momentum you have lost.

I hope this book inspires you to make that commitment to change your future and to become enormously successful financially and clinically, in dentistry. You can have one of the most successful and elite dental practices in the nation, if you so desire, and you can have an enormous amount of fun being ultra-successful.

If you are at the point in your life where you are ready to make the income you deserve, and build the practice of your dreams, then give us a call for a free consultation to see if Quantum Leap Success in Dentistry is right for you.

Dr. Mike Kesner

Chapter One

What Do You Want?

Dentistry is a wonderful profession, but it is also a very difficult profession. As a practicing dentist, I guess I don't need to tell you that. There can be a lot of stress involved in diagnosing, treatment planning, selling, and then performing the necessary dentistry that your patient needs. If you've been practicing for years, then you probably have the typical dentist's neck, shoulder and back pain caused from hours and hours of leaning over patients' mouths.

But, one of the many great things about dentistry is that we are in control of the type of practice we want to have, and even the level of success that we want to have.

You can have a solo practice or have multiple doctors. You can have partners and/or associate dentists. You can have multiple locations. You can get the education and add implants or cosmetic dentistry or orthodontics or TMJ treatment to your practice and dramatically change your income.

You can implement proven systems, techniques and strategies that will make you and your practice much more profitable. There are not many other professions out there that give these types of opportunities for success.

Over the years, I have noticed how there are a few practices that are very successful and do so much better than most other practices with only average success.

There are a few practices that seem to get more than their fair share of success. Why is that?

These practices seem to have enormous success financially and clinically. These doctors are able to grow large practices fairly quick, while others around them seemed to be struggling financially.

There are keys, principles, systems and techniques which make multi-million-dollar dental practices. The good news is that these can all be learned and implemented by any dentist who is willing to make the changes.

**The unusual thing is that many
of these principles of success
are counter-intuitive.**

Many of these counter-intuitive keys, to great success in dental practice, elude dentists and keep them from attaining the multi-million-dollar success.

**<u>You too can become wealthy
in dentistry. It is simply
a matter of choice.</u>**

I know that sounds too simple, but it's not. You can have enormous success in dentistry if that is what you want. It is going to require change on your part, new skills and new learning, but you can have a multi-million-dollar practice, if you want a multi-million-dollar practice. You can net $1 million a year in dentistry, if that is what you want.

You can have pretty much anything you want in life if you are willing to pay the price that it requires. Some dentists, who are not clients of Quantum Leap Success in Dentistry, will talk with me and tell me that they want to build a multi-million-dollar practice. I will ask them a few questions about their practice and make some suggestions of changes they can make to increase their revenue. Sometimes they will say... "No, I can't change that." – or – "I don't what to change the way I do this."

I then tell them that they really don't want a multi-million-dollar practice after all. They think they do, but their response, of refusing to change, really confirms the fact that they value their comfort, and their unwillingness to change is more valuable to them than building a multi-million-dollar practice. You can have the practice of your dreams if you are willing to commit to do whatever it takes to make it happen.

Deciding what you want is half the battle. For most of us it is easier to decide what we <u>don't want</u> instead of what we <u>do want.</u>

Most of us go through life doing what other people want us to do or expect us to do. We may have spent our lives doing what our parents wanted us to do or what someone else in authority over us wanted; therefore, it is sometimes hard for us to get back to what we really want for ourselves. What is your dream? What would you do with your life if money and time were no object?

We have to get in touch with our real dreams and passions. What do you love to do? What are you passionate about? What is it that you do that "turns your crank"? What thing or things do you get lost in and time seems to fly by? What do you enjoy talking about so much that others wish you would shut up? These will give you clues to what your passions are.

Once you discover your passions...the things that drive you,...then you can start dreaming and setting goals that are in line with those passions. This leads to a life that is full and complete.

Every one of us has something that God has placed inside of us that we love to do.

It is the thing or things that we are naturally good at and they fit with our gifts and our talents perfectly. When we are functioning in this place, then we feel the most alive. This is where your deepest dreams and desires for your life reside. If you are not sure what those are for you, ask God to show you and He will.

The big question is...What if your passions, dreams and desires are not dentistry?

Oh crap!! Just kidding.

The great thing is that dentistry can be the vehicle to help you live out your passions, dreams and desires. In other words, you can develop a practice that is so successful it will fund and provide a way for you to do the thing or things you are really passionate about. This is one of the truly wonderful things about our profession. - The freedom to create the type of practice that meets the needs of your life and provides the avenue to do what you are really passionate about.

Being hugely successful in dentistry can be your destiny in life, or it can provide a means to your destiny in life. Not many other professions have the ability to do that.

Many dentists, or people in general for that matter, don't find their way to this kind of success in life. Surveys show us that most dentists don't like what they do, don't make enough money doing it and would switch careers if they could afford to, financially.

In the 1980's a survey was done of dentists, which found that 67% of those surveyed wished they had not become a dentist. I believe that statistic is higher today than it was then

Surveys also show us that only around 3% of dentists can retire at the same standard of living they are used to,

and many cannot afford to retire at all.

Would making a million dollars a year in your practice help these statistics? I think it would. I know that I didn't like dentistry very much when I was only making $120,000 a year. In my opinion, dentistry is much too hard, and the risk of owning your own business is much too high for that level of income.

Let's take a look at a few of the risks and responsibilities you take as an owner dentist. First of all you had 4-5 years of undergraduate education followed by 4 years in dental school. This is 8-9 years of higher education, not counting any residency or specialty training. Most dentists today graduate from dental school with hundreds of thousands of dollars in school debt which will take them years to pay off.

If you start your own practice from scratch or purchase an existing practice, then you now have become a small business owner. Your name is on the note with the bank, which means you are assuming a large financial risk.

As a small business owner you wear a lot of "hats". First you must run a business with all the responsibilities of being an employer. There are withholding tax, FICA tax, state taxes, unemployment tax, franchise tax, federal and state filing requirements, hiring, firing, discipline, vacation, sick days, raises, vendors to pay, budgets to make, marketing decisions, etc. You also have your employees and their families counting on your success for their income.

Another "hat" is managing your overhead and understanding profit and loss statements and balance sheets and having to make appropriate business decisions based upon this information. You now have CPA and attorney fees to pay as you navigate through the sea of rules, regulations and laws that you now must abide by.

Then there is malpractice risk. It used to be that dentists almost never got sued. Then it was 1 in 10 dentists got sued every year...then 1 in 8...and now I think the number is 1 in 7. The trend is changing to where it is not IF you will get sued, but WHEN you will get sued.

On top of all of this, you have to be an excellent clinician and stay up on top of all that is new in dentistry, which is continually changing with the rapid technological advancements today. This means traveling to continuing education courses with the associated expense of tuition, air fare, hotel and meals.

If all of this weren't enough, dentistry itself is very difficult. We work on a scared patient in a small dark wet hole with a tongue that is constantly trying to get in the way. We contort our bodies to simultaneously hold the mirror, hold the handpiece, keep the soft tissue out of the way, see in a mirror while water is blowing all over it or while the patient is fogging it up with their breath. You must also keep the light in the right spot while the patient is not doing a very good job of holding still.

Now you must place a restoration that will succeed or fail based upon microns, that must stand up to 1000 pounds per square inch of force 24/7, that will probably not get cleaned very well, and should last for several years. We are counting on the restoration lasting 10 - 15 years while the patient is counting on it lasting forever. (Doesn't it seem funny that people can screw up what God gave them, but what we give them is supposed to last forever!?)

I know I am being a little facetious, but you can only fully relate to this if you are a dentist. The general public has no concept of how hard we work to do what we do in people's mouths.

I believe that when you take into account all of these risks, responsibilities and challenges you assume as a small business owner and a clinician, a compensation of $120,000 or $200,000 or even $500,000 a year is not a level of compensation that is commensurate with the risk assumed.

This needs to change.

As a consultant, we are in dentist's offices all across the nation. We find two things to be universally true.

1. Most dentists don't make the income they deserve.
2. Most dentists don't know what to do to change number 1.

We find that dentists really do want to change their level of income, but they have no idea where to start. Should they hire more staff or let some staff go? Should they market more, or change their marketing, or just give up on marketing. Maybe they need to buy a new laser or CAD/CAM to solve their problems. Should they work longer hours, or work less hours since things have slowed down? Should they hire a consultant, and if so, which one? Should they take in some more CE courses on new procedures, or will this pay off since their number of new patients is way down? Should they cut back on hygiene days, or try to get hygiene back to where it used to be? Etc., etc.

Our new economy has made these questions harder to answer and even more confusing for the doctor. The rules for success in dentistry have changed in this down economy. You cannot practice dentistry like you used to and expect to be successful. We live in a different world now.

Changing your level of success in dentistry may be the most important thing for you to accomplish in your life right now. Why? Because changing your level of success to earn the income you deserve can be the key to realizing and revitalizing your passions and your dreams. Being passionate about dentistry is difficult when you are not successful. I am far more passionate about dentistry and the business of dentistry now, than when I was poor dentist.

Once you discover your passions and dreams... Then what? You have to make a decision – a commitment to do whatever it takes to realize your dreams. Why? If you don't live your dreams, then you are not going to live your life to the fullest. You have to make this all-or-nothing kind of commitment because you are going to have to make changes in the way you do things, which will be uncomfortable at first.

If what you are doing now was working, then you would be getting different results. Therefore, making changes in your life is necessary and usually uncomfortable for most of us.

If you are not passionate about what you are doing, then you won't have sufficient drive to have the "do-whatever-it-takes" commitment level. Passion is what pushes you and drives you through the "uncomfortableness" of change.

You are also going to have to endure some difficulties along the way. Success never comes to us on a trouble-free silver platter. There are some bumps in the road and some setbacks that come, in order to make us better and stronger people. There are always challenges and roadblocks that we have to figure a way over and around. If you don't have this "all-or-nothing" kind of commitment level, then you won't have the sufficient perseverance to carry you through the difficult times.

This is why discovering your dreams and passions is so important. When we learn to operate our lives from this level, then we tap into a source of power that is the foundation of who we are and who we were meant to be. In other words, you start to tap into your destiny and your purpose in life.

**When we function at this level,
there is a power and drive that
is stronger than the adversities
we will encounter on our journey
to our dreams and goals.**

Now, we can set the goals we need to set to accomplish the dreams that tap into who we are and what God put us here to do. The keys to that reality are found in our passions and our dreams.

How successful do you really want to be in dentistry? How bad do you want it? Are you willing to make a "do whatever it takes" commitment?

**We all have to get to the point
in our lives, where the place we
currently are is more uncomfortable
than the change necessary to get
to the place we want to be.**

It took me 19 years to get to that place of being uncomfortable enough with my lack of financial success in dentistry, to make the changes necessary for that success to occur.

I decided that I would change whatever I needed to change in myself. I decided that I would fire whatever employees I needed to fire. I decided that I would hire whatever coaches and consultants that I needed to hire. I decided that I would do whatever kind of marketing I needed to do, in order to bring in the number of patients I needed to bring in. I decided that I would build whatever facility I needed to build. I decided that I would learn and do whatever was necessary to gain the speed and clinical excellence I needed to be profitable.

<u>You can do it!</u> To reach your goals, it is going to require a lot of change in what you do in your practice and how you do it.

Huge success in dentistry eludes most dentists because they are not willing to do whatever is necessary to get there. I am of course not talking about doing anything that is illegal, unethical or against your state board rules and regulations. I am also of course not talking about doing poor dentistry.

One of the biggest and hardest changes you will have to make, on your journey to practice success, is changing the way you think. Our biggest challenge to success is what goes on between our ears. We all have beliefs, thoughts and behavioral "hang ups" that keep us from being successful.

I find that, when doctors are confronted with these "hang ups," they sometimes get defensive and make justifications or denials that these problems exists. Remember, the hardest things to change are yourself and the way you think and relate to the world. Your success in your practice will always be stunted until you decide to change.

I find that many dentists spend an enormous amount of energy making excuses for their lack of success, and how this lack of success is not their fault.

They explain away other dentist's success as being lucky, or being in a better area than they are, or having better business skills, or the dentists are lying about their success, or even that the successful dentists are "crossing the line" clinically. I get these and other judgments from dentists, sometimes. It is as if these dentists feel better about their lack of success when they are bashing the dentists that are very successful.

I used to be that way. It is amazing when you think about how much money that kind of thinking costs you.

This kind of thinking keeps you stuck where you are. When you "shoot down" others who are successful, you are sabotaging your own success.

It is a fact that, when we make negative judgments about other people, we doom ourselves to do what we are judging them for.

We have all seen this biblical principle in action. How many politicians and tele-evangelists have we seen who have publically judged others for sexual immorality and/or lack of integrity? After several

15

months went by, these same politicians and evangelists were caught doing what they were judging others for.

How about an example that is a little closer to home? How many of us have judged our parents for one thing or another? We then make the statement... "I'll never be like my father." – or – "I'll never be like my mother." Then we find ourselves saying and/or doing to our children the same things that we judged our parents for doing to us. Ouch!

Believe me, you will never be successful in dentistry if you continually criticize and judge those that are successful in dentistry.

You are putting negative energy out there which brings nothing good to you. Criticizing other dentists' success is really just a ploy to take the focus off your own problems and put the blame on someone else.

I used to live this way. I judged other dentists' success. I judged other dentists' clinical abilities. I even judged clinical treatment philosophies that I disagreed with, by writing critical articles of these techniques. These judgments came back to bite me in a big way. I even went through a few years of fighting with other dentists over treatment philosophies. Nothing good came out of this, other than stroking my ego and hurting the ego of other doctors. Is there any wonder that I was not successful until I changed this behavior? The way I changed this behavior was by changing the false beliefs behind the behavior.

Whatever we believe, on a deep level, will determine our behavior. In other words, our thoughts about things in life come from our deeply held beliefs. These thoughts then lead to our actions.

If some of our deeply held beliefs are false, which many are, then this will lead to wrong thoughts which lead to wrong actions.

Let me give you an example. My parents grew up very poor and in very large families. My grandparents passed on belief systems to my parents, which no doubt came from their parents. One false belief was that being wealthy was somehow unspiritual and wrong. The false belief was that rich people have done something wrong to achieve the wealth they have.

There was also an additional false belief that God somehow likes poor people more than He likes rich people.

This was a non-verbal, deeply held belief, which was, to be really loved by God, you needed to be poor. There were always scriptures taken out of context and wrongly interpreted, to substantiate this false belief. Would it surprise you to know that many of Jesus' disciples were wealthy? You don't hear that one in church much do you?

I have spent a lot of time in third world countries, with the poor. I can tell you that the poor in America are rich in comparison to the poor in other countries. So, guess what? Compared to the rest of the world, we in America are all rich! Did you know that if you make more than $29,000 a year, then you are in the top 1% of the wealthiest people in the world? That fact can really mess with this false belief system.

For years I tried to become wealthy in my practice, but looking back I can see that time-after-time I did things to self-sabotage my own success.

The result of my false belief about wealth was to subconsciously self-sabotage my success. Even though I desperately wanted success in my dental practice, no matter how hard I tried, I would always do something bone-headed to sabotage my success. I see this behavior all the time in other dentists.

This blockage to success came from my deeply held false belief that it was wrong to be wealthy. I had to first realize this false belief was there, and then make the effort to exchange this false belief with the truth.

This is something you need to get in touch with yourself, because if you don't believe you deserve wealth, or you believe it is wrong to be rich, then you will never be successful in your practice. You will self-sabotage your success to keep your external reality congruent with your deeply held beliefs.

Do you ever say things like; "He is filthy rich." -- or-- "He has money coming out of the wazoo." -- because of the false belief that money is dirty. "This is my hard earned money."-- because of the false belief that money only comes to us the hard way. "I wonder where he came up with all his money?"-- because of the false belief that to have a lot of money means he must have done something illegal or unethical to get it.

I find that many people I talk to don't realize their lack of success is something they have created, and that they also have the power to create something different.

They don't realize that their lack of success is something they have caused, and that they have the ability and the control in their lives to change it. Dentists typically blame their staff, or the economy, or the type of people in their town, or their location, or their competition, or whatever.

The condition you find yourself in is a product of your deeply held belief systems and you have the power to change that. You may need help from a person you trust who will "tell you like it is" and then walk with you through the change.

The false belief about money is just one of the many false beliefs which in turn lead to wrong thoughts, which in turn lead to wrong actions, which in turn inhibits your success. Identify the false belief, exchange it with the truth and your thoughts will change, which will cause your actions to change, which will cause your reality to change.

You need to realize that, whatever situation your practice is in, and whatever financial situation you presently find yourself in was created by you. You can re-create something different.

Don't blame everyone else. The sooner you realize the problem is you, the sooner you can take a hard look in the mirror and make the necessary changes.

Do you want to be "right" or do you want to be rich? It is your choice.

The good news is that you can make the necessary changes if you want success bad enough. The hardest thing in achieving my success was changing false beliefs that inhibited that success.

Statistically only one out of one hundred people in any profession will achieve above average success. The interesting thing is that this 1% doesn't know some secret information that the other 99% don't know. So, what makes the difference in their results? Why does this one enjoy above average success when the other 99 don't?

There are four things that every person who accomplishes above average success does, regardless of their profession. If you will do these four things, I can guarantee that you can make your practice be in the top 1% in the nation.

1. Believe that you can do it.

Remember, the most important thing in life is what you believe. – Whatever you believe is right - because, what you believe creates your reality!

21

If you believe that you <u>can't</u> build a multi-million-dollar practice, then you are right! You can't!

If you believe that you <u>can</u> build a multi-million-dollar practice, then you are right! You can!

If you believe that the economy is in control of your success, then you are right! It is!

If you believe that <u>you</u> are in control of your success, then you are right! You are!

You create your reality with your thoughts which are rooted in your beliefs.

Your beliefs determine your thoughts, which determine your actions, which determine your results.

What you believe, is the most important thing in the world. What do you really believe about you and your ability to change your reality to something you want? If you want to change your reality just change your beliefs!

Decide what you really want for you, your family and your practice. Believe that you can do it. Watch your reality change.

You created the reality you presently have. You can therefore create a different reality. It is simply a matter of belief.

2. Do whatever it takes.

After the orthodontist that bought my practice was killed, I decided to do whatever it took to build a multi-million-dollar practice. Why? Because I did not want to go back to being a poor dentist again. I had spent too many years "just getting by", and I was determined to never go back to that place again.

You have to find something that motivates to you "do whatever it takes" because the journey is not going to be easy. Determination to never go back to "just getting by", and a burning desire for success were my motivations. What are your motivations?

Find what motivates you to "do whatever it takes", and use that to build the practice of your dreams.

3. Hire someone who has been there before and can show you the way.

Every successful business person or athlete has a mentor, or consultant, or coach. For instance, look at the TV show "The Apprentice". The contestants on this reality show are already successful business people who are willing to do whatever it takes to be able to work under Donald Trump. Why? Because Mr. Trump knows how to create huge success in business and real estate, and the contestants want that opportunity for mentoring.

Tiger Woods is the best golfer in the world, and possibly of all time. He has won 14 major golf championships, 71 PGA tournaments, 16 world championships and is the youngest player to win a Grand Slam.

He has a coach.

Roger Federer is the number one men's singles tennis player in the world. He is widely considered the best tennis player of all time. He has played in 22 Grand Slam tournaments and has won a record 16 of them.

He has a coach.

Why do the most successful business people and athletes have coaches or mentors when they are obviously already successful? Because you can't see what is hindering your own success. You need someone who has been there before that can show you the way. You need someone to point out to you the things that need changing to reach your objective. You can't see these things…the coach can.

4. Take massive action.

The secret to success is not in the knowledge of information, but in the implementation of that information. This requires action.

When we take on a dentist as a client it becomes obvious very quickly if he is going to have quantum leap growth or just a little growth. The dentists who always have quantum leap growth are the ones who are willing to take our recommended action, and do it quickly and completely.

The dentists that have limited success believe they know better than their consultant, and they pick and choose what action they are going to take and not take. They usually believe their situation is totally unique and unlike anything the consultant has seen before. Also, the dentists who keep putting off taking action out of fear or laziness have limited success.

All people that experience above average success, determine what action needs to happen with the help of their coach/consultant. Then they take that action quickly and decisively.

If you do all of these above four things in your business life, I guarantee that you will build the practice of your dreams.

Your level of success really is simply a matter of choice.

Chapter Two

The Average Dentist Today

One of my passions and dreams is to change the present condition of dentistry today, by helping dentists to change their financial future. As I said earlier, dentistry is a great profession which provides wonderful opportunities that many other professions can't and don't provide. We have opportunities for income levels that are better than most professions - even medicine.

We can accomplish high levels of success, working only 4 days a week or even less, with huge monthly increases in our incomes just by changing the way we do a few things in our practices.

Most other businesses don't have the high profit margins we do. They also don't have the "monopoly" we enjoy, since in most states only a dentist can own a dental practice. Most businesses also don't have a "product" that every person has a need for, like we enjoy in dentistry.

A study was recently done by Sageworks, Inc. identifying the most profitable industries for 2008. Dentistry was number one! Number two was accounting firms, followed by legal services, followed by health practitioners.

I agree that dentistry itself is very difficult to do well. It takes years to become a "master craftsman", and then to be able to do it in a time efficient manner, without quality suffering. I once heard Dr. Gordon Christensen say; "As dentists we learn how to do dentistry very well, and then we die."

I think that the personalities of most of us dentists are such that we learn to do the clinical aspects of dentistry very well, and are proud of our work. The problem that I find is that they stop there and never learn how to be very profitable and successful with their clinical excellence.

**In other words, dentists become good
at the clinical part of dentistry, but
not at the business part of dentistry.**

Let's take a look at the statistics of the average U.S. dentist. The average dentist is 54 years old and does not enjoy his career choice. He has experienced three gut wrenching malpractice lawsuits in his 27 year career. Statistically, most of these lawsuits have been frivolous, from patients that had an unfavorable outcome, which was not the fault of the dentist, but made the patient angry enough and the attorney was hungry enough to sue.

After these 27 years in dentistry, the 54 year old dentist has $225,000 in retirement funds, which he knows is not going to be enough for him to retire.

He has no idea how he is going to grow the $225K to the $3 million he will need to retire at the same standard of living he presently has. The reason he has not been able to save enough is because he only has a net-before-taxes income of only $127,780 per year.

He only sees around 22 new patients per month with a case average of only $1000. This number reflects his inability to get patients to do the dentistry he diagnoses.

He works a total of 1806 hours per year which is equal to 225 days per year, for an hourly income before taxes of $70.75 per hour. This is about double what he pays his hygienist per hour, and only slightly more than what a typical plumber makes per hour.

**I don't think this is acceptable!
Dentistry is way too hard and has far
too much risk for this level of success.**

The good news is that your numbers can be changed, and changed quickly. I did it and so can you. You will need help but you can change this! This control over your destiny is one of the things that is so wonderful about the business of dentistry.

**One of the questions I get from
dentists all the time is, "How are you
able to do the numbers you do"?**

They then stand there and expect me to answer that question in one or two sentences. There is a false belief amongst dentists that there are just one or two secrets to building a multi-million-dollar dental practice. Their hope is that I can tell them these one or two secrets, which they can go home and try, and their practice will immediately be transformed.

**My answer is that there are not just
one or two secrets; there are about
"50 secrets" which have to be implemented
in the right way and in the right order
to work together synergistically to**

produce extra-ordinary results.

When I say this, I usually get blank looks which non-verbally say... "What in the hell are you talking about?" I think that some of them are thinking that I am intentionally withholding information just to be mean.

These 50 or so "secrets" to success are not linear and are not the same for everyone, and these "secrets" are often counter-intuitive. In other words, sometimes the problem is the inability to do effective case presentations. This process actually starts with the initial phone call and ends with the financial coordinator an hour or so later after the new patient comes for their appointment.

Maybe the problem is that the front desk ladies do not know how to effectively "close the sale" and get a prospective new patient caller scheduled. Maybe the problem is a doctor that believes patients make their decisions about whether or not to do treatment, based upon education instead of emotion. Maybe the problem is not knowing how to connect with the patient on an emotional level.

Maybe the problem is that the team is not empowered to "sell" the necessary dental treatment to patients, when the doctor is not in the room.

Maybe the problem is that the doctor is talking too much and talking patients out of treatment, instead of into it.

Maybe the problem is not enough of the right kind of marketing to bring in a sufficient number of new patients per month.

Maybe the problem is presenting too much treatment to the patient too soon and "blowing them away". Maybe the problem is that the staff has not been incentivized financially. Maybe the problem is not having the right staff. Maybe the problem is not creating urgency with new patients. Maybe the problem is not enough capacity in the way of treatment rooms, assistants, front desk people and/ or hygienists. Maybe the problem is not trusting the staff to run the daily operations of the practice better than you can, which causes you to micro-manage everything.

Maybe the problem is not having any idea where to look for the problems.
Maybe the problem is all of the above and more (which is usually the case).

What I am saying is that there are a lot of moving parts to a high performance car. If any one of those moving parts is not functioning properly, then the performance of that car suffers. The problem is that you don't know which part of the engine needs to be tuned up, over-hauled or replaced since you are not a mechanic. Once the mechanic (consultant) gets under the hood and fixes what needs to be fixed, then the engine starts performing in the way it was designed. You can go from 0 to 60 mph in 3-5 seconds! The same is true for a dental practice.

You can go from $750,000 per year in collections to over $3 million per year in collections, in 3-5 years.

I am going to be real honest with you. Most dentists...myself included...are "do-it-yourselfers" and we are usually cheap. I am always fighting this about myself. I usually default to trying to find the cheap way around doing something which usually comes back to bite me in the butt. Many times I think I can do it myself and save some money but, if I would have delegated it to someone else, I would have saved time, money and had a much better result. Dumb!

Many times, when dentists are trying to change the success in their practice, they will try to fix the problem by themselves. Many dentists try to fix a problem by thinking the way they are comfortable thinking, which is clinically. They think that they can fix their lack of success by purchasing a new high dollar piece of equipment like a laser or a CAD-CAM machine or a digital impression gadget.

There is nothing wrong with cutting-edge equipment, but new patients are not going to be falling over each other trying to get through your front door because you now have a new laser.

Nor are they going to run to your practice and accept whatever treatment you recommend because you got a new fish tank, or a fancy coffee machine, or free Wi-Fi internet in your waiting room.

There is nothing wrong with having these things in our practices, but they are not going to bring you the success you want and need. The problem is not that you don't have a salt water aquarium or a CAD/CAM, the problem is that you need help with your systems, your staff, your scheduling, your marketing and your personal hang-ups which keep you from success.

But, it feels easier and smarter for us to make the financial investment in a fancy new piece of dental equipment than to make the financial investment in an experienced dental practice coach or consultant.

The amount of money you will invest in a coach or consultant, to get you to where you want to be, will pay for itself thousands of times over. If you could have quantum leap growth by yourself, then you already would have!

You need the advice and input from others that have already "been there and done that". They can see things about you and your practice that are sabotaging your success, which you can't see. They can also give you the proper solution for the problems and even help you implement them.

You can't see the problems which are keeping you from huge success.

Yet, you keep passing over wealth that you could be making because you are too scared to spend the money necessary to get a good consultant and coach. I know that I am being bluntly honest, but I can talk to you this way because I was there myself. I also see this mentality in many of the dentists I come in contact with.

However, don't make the mistake of hiring a dental consultant that has only "read the book" and has not already achieved the level of success you aspire to. The proof really is in the pudding. You need someone that has been there and can show you the way.

Let me spend the next few chapters giving you some of the "secrets" to a thriving multi-million dollar recession proof practice that will net you $1 million or more per year.

You have to promise me...like they say on TV... "Don't try this at home by yourself"!

Read on as I discuss some of the "50 secrets" to a multi-million-dollar practice. I am going to be giving you glimpses into some of the "secrets" that make a multi-million-dollar practice which will net you $1 million per year. Keep in mind that these are just glimpses. My purpose in this book is not to give you 13 chapters to guaranteed success, because that is not possible. My purpose is also not to give you a few tricks that you can implement to build a multi-million-dollar practice, because that is not possible either.

My purpose is to get you to believe that, if I did and am still doing it right now, then I can help you do it too! As you can see in Chapter 13, we have lots of clients that have built the practice of their dreams. You can also check out our website at www.qlsuccess.com, and hear doctors talk about the quantum leap growth in their practices.

Chapter Three

A Team With The Right Stuff

A great team of employees that work for you and with you is vital to your success. They have to understand your vision and goals for the practice and take them on as their own. Their function is more like a business partner than an employee.

A business partner understands how the success of the business impacts their own success. A business partner doesn't think or say..."That's not my job", but looks at what needs to be done and gets it done. A business partner doesn't look to you to figure everything out, but takes the initiative to come up with a solution when they see a problem without being told to do so. A business partner enjoys taking on responsibilities and does not respond well to micro-management.

You need business partners not employees to build a multi-million dollar practice. Business partners will make your life easier. Employees will make your life stressful.

There is no way that I could have had the success that I enjoy now without a great team of business partners working with me. Presently, I have a team leader, five at the front desk, a hygiene coordinator, five dental assistants, two hygiene assistants, three hygienists, and one associate dentist. All of these people have to be up to speed with where the practice is going and what our daily, weekly, monthly, quarterly and annual goals are.

You need to realize that a great team is a necessity for your success, but your success does not hinge on any single individual member of your team. It truly is a team and must function as a team, so you must realize that your success will not rise or fall on any one person, except yourself.

Sometimes, I run across dentists who feel like they are being held hostage by a particular staff member. The dentist and this staff member have come to a false belief that the practice cannot survive or succeed without this staff member's presence.

This attitude usually hinders the rest of the team because it makes them feel second-rate and/ or resentful. This attitude also causes this particular staff member to get away with behavior that the rest of the team cannot get away with. This damages morale and therefore the success of the practice.

Doctor, you need to realize that your success is ultimately determined by you and not by others. It may be rough for a while to do without a particular "queen bee" staff member, but that person does not dictate your success. You do. But, to have a multimillion-dollar practice, you must have a very strong and empowered team.

One of the major things that keeps my team strong and empowered is a bonus system that is tied to the profitability of the practice.

This bonus system allows the staff to receive a monthly percentage of the profit of the practice. I don't believe it is fair of us to ask our team to work harder and smarter yet not receive something in return. This bonus system rewards them and keeps them very focused on the profitability and the overhead of the office.

**The amount of bonus that your
team receives has to be an
amount that really makes
a difference in their lives.**

My team receives a monthly bonus on top of their salary that typically ranges from 50 to 100% of their monthly salary. This is a substantial amount of money each month, but it is not costing me anything because the staff is always pushing and running the practice and keeping me busy.

In other words, if the financial incentive was not there, then I would not be enjoying the profits, from the practice, that I enjoy. Therefore, it is only fair that I should give them a percentage of the monthly company's profits. You may be thinking that you don't have any monthly profits to share. Once you get all the "50 secrets" in place, you will have more than enough to share.

The regular salary that my team receives is for their normal job duties. It is important that your staff understands this principle. Their regular salary is for coming to work on time, getting along with the rest of the team, taking good care of the patients, and doing their regular duties and responsibilities.

**Their bonus is for work that is
above and beyond the normal**

level of performance.

The bonus is for learning better ways to communicate with patients, for better results. It is for getting that "same day dentistry" worked into the schedule to get our daily production numbers up. The bonus is for learning our systems and taking on responsibilities that require them to think and problem solve, as opposed to waiting for someone else to figure it out.

The bonus is for all the extra things they do, as a motivated team, that make a multi-million-dollar practice stay a multi-million-dollar practice.

A bonus system that works for you and the employees is an essential part of your success. A proper bonus system gives an incentive to the employees to work hard, to work smart, to handle many of the practice's day-to-day challenges and to also have a feeling of ownership in the practice.

The bonus system has to be designed right. I have seen many bonus systems that turn out to be dis-incentives instead of incentives.

The bonus system cannot be designed in a way that the goal is so far out there that they rarely reach it. It must also not be so top heavy that it is costing the practice too much. It is important to have a bonus system that is based upon a percentage of the profit of the practice. As the practice grows and the overhead grows, the bonus system must account for this and adjust the baseline overhead figure from which the percentage of profit is figured.

The bonus system also eliminates pay raises for the employees. Once a person is hired on at a particular salary, this salary typically never changes. Pay raises happen as the practice grows and becomes more and more profitable.

My team makes far more in bonuses than they would ever make in pay raises. They get a pay raise when the doctor gets a pay raise which is as the practice makes more and more profit.

If your practice revenues are flat, or even worse they are declining, then raises for your employees are funds that are coming out of your take home pay. They get a cost of living raise, and you get a decrease in your take home income. This is not fair.

**It is very important that you,
as the doctor, be the biggest
cheerleader of the bonus.**

If the staff senses that you are begrudgingly paying their monthly bonus, then you will turn the bonus into a dis-incentive. Most everything that happens in the practice is tied to the bonus. In other words, when we have staff meetings, we talk about what we can do to increase the bonus.

How can we serve patients better to increase the bonus? How can we tweak our systems to make them more efficient to increase the bonus? When do we need to hire a new staff person to increase our productivity to cause the bonus to increase?

Now you have a team that is working with you toward a common goal, which is to increase their bonus. You now have a business partner!

Remember that, as their bonus increases, so does yours! Without a working bonus system, the team will resist changes that you want to make in the practice, because you are asking them to work harder and smarter, but not compensating them for their added efforts. How would you as the dentist like to work harder and see more patients, but not see any change in your income? (That sounds like managed care plans!)

Another really powerful thing that happens, with a good bonus system, is that the employees begin to start taking care of problems with other employees who are not "pulling their weight".

When a team member is not doing their fair share of the work, yet that team member is sharing equally in the bonus, this does not set well with the rest of the team. The team will take control of this situation and talk with that particular team member.

Things either change or they recommend that this particular employee be terminated. This takes a huge responsibility off the doctor's plate of things he must do. The performance problems of that employee suddenly become the team's problem to solve and not yours.

I have found that the "slacking" team member usually responds much better to their peer's criticism than from the doctor's criticism. It is easy for the offending team member to justify their problem as just criticism from an over-demanding doctor. This is not an easy argument to make when the criticism is coming from the rest of the team.

When a new employee is hired, that person has a two to three month probationary period before they can take part in the bonus plan, and before the base overhead is increased by their particular salary. This gives the rest of the team a few months to get this new employee "up to speed" so their presence is increasing the overall production of the practice and therefore keeping everyone's bonus the same or pushing it higher. The team understands that the only reason to hire an employee is to increase the capacity and profitability of the practice, as opposed to hiring someone just to make their work load easier.

I expect a lot from my team and they work very hard. They like the sense of control they have over their own monthly paycheck. This is empowering to them and an empowered team is a team you can put your trust in to help take your practice to the level you want it to be.

The team also realizes that their income level is far above what other dental offices are paying their employees, which helps to keep them loyal to your practice.

Another thing we do to incentivize the team is to have quarterly collection goals. When we hit these quarterly collection goals three months in a row, then we do something special. I will typically rent the biggest limo I can find and stock it with Champagne and take them on a shopping spree. I will give them around $300 each and they have two hours to spend every dime of it on themselves.

One time I rented a whole spa and the team spent the day having massages, manicures and pedicures. These times are lots of fun and really get the team focused on pushing the practice to that next level. This is a great reward for all the hard work they do. These times are also great for building stronger relationships amongst the team members.

Another part of the bonus system is the continuing education part. Each month 10% of the total bonus amount is put into a CE account and I match that 10% each month. This account builds up a large amount of funds which we use once or twice a year to travel to a nice continuing education event. Again, just another thing that keeps the team motivated and energized.

We are always looking for good people. We are continuously interviewing because we are continuing to grow. Team members get married and move, or a spouse gets transferred and you lose a team member. Often times, when we have an employee leave, we feel like we have to fill that spot ASAP since we are short-handed. This can lead to us hiring the wrong person because we are in a hurry.

That is why we are always looking for good people. Many times, if you find someone great and you are not quite ready to hire them, they will be willing to wait a few months until you are ready because they realize what a great opportunity this is for them.

One thing that is very important for the health of your practice is to fire employees quickly if the need arises. A toxic team member can drain everyone and really do some damage to your practice.

I have hung onto employees before because they were fantastic in their skills and job performance but they were toxic to the morale and attitudes of the rest of the staff. I once had a staff member that had been threatening other staff members for several months in a desire to maintain control over them. The other team members were so afraid of her that they would not speak up.

I had another team member once that would not come under the authority of the team leader and would passive-aggressively undermine her authority and then try to get the other team members to do the same.

Both of these employees were some of the best I have ever had in their skills and in taking care of the patients as well, but their dysfunctional behaviors were damaging to the morale of the other team members and it took focus away from our purpose. Remember, there is no one team member that you can't live without, no matter how good they are.

You have to decide to fire quickly.

**I have never regretted firing a person,
but I have regretted hanging on to
the wrong person for too long. You
may have heard the statement...
"You can't change people, but you
can change people ."**

Don't hang onto an employee thinking that you are going to be able to change their dysfunctional behavior. You are in the business of dentistry not psychology. Change that person for another one. "Free up their future" and hire a new team member that is right for your practice.

I have found that, when I remove a toxic employee, the practice takes a tremendous jump in production. It is like we reach a ceiling we can't break through, which was because of the behavioral turmoil that a toxic employee brings to the rest of the team.

Now, let's talk about the ways to compensate your hygienists. Hygienists have a somewhat different position on the team in the practice, since they are producers. They are <u>not</u> a more important part of the team but, since they are producers, their compensation needs to be different than the rest of the team.

I am a firm believer in paying hygienists on commission. I have paid hourly, salary and commission and I can tell you that commission is a huge win-win situation for everyone. My hygienists, and I, would never go back to a salary.

When your hygienists are on commission, you will be amazed at how much your hygiene production will increase.

Your hygienists will also be amazed at how much their income will increase.

Going on commission is a scary thing for most hygienists. They are afraid that their income may go down and are afraid to take that risk. What you can do to make this transition to commission easy, is to give your hygienist the "best of" either salary (or hourly if this is how you presently pay your hygienist) or commission for 6 months.

This will give them a period of time to prove to themselves that they will make far more money on commission than on salary. My hygienists make about as much per month as many dentists make in a typical practice.

The power of commission is that you basically pay the hygienist around 1/3 of their monthly collections, the second 1/3 of the collections goes to pay the hygiene overhead and the last 1/3 goes to you, the dentist.

When you decide to put your hygienist on commission, you as the doctor have to step up and guarantee some support.

You are asking the hygienist to take a risk here, so you need to take a risk too and provide a person that is dedicated to keeping the hygiene schedule full and possibly hire a hygiene assistant.

With an assistant, your hygienist will be able to see around twice the number of patients they normally see because they won't have to be setting up the room, taking x-rays, cleaning the room, doing periodontal charting measurements by themselves and charting existing dentistry, etc.

Remember, the more patients they can see, the more dentistry you are going to be able to diagnose.

If you double the number of exams you do each day in re-call patients and new patients, then it stands to reason that you will diagnose twice the dentistry.

This is a quick way to greatly increase your production, pay your hygienist more and make about twice as much as you were from your hygiene department. This is a great win-win all the way around. Your hygiene department will then start generating around 30% of your total collections and be a profit center for your practice. In most practices the hygiene department is a loss leader.

You can't have a multi-million-dollar practice without a great team. You also can't have a multi-million-dollar practice without a great team leader.

My team leader runs the practice. She keeps me focused on the dentistry. We meet often and I set the vision, goals and agendas for the practice and she carries them out. There is no way I could do this without her. At this level of production, you must have a team leader that has your trust and authority to hire, fire, interview, and discipline the team. They need to have your trust to take care of the day-to-day operations of the office. The busier I get, the lower my stress gets because of a great team leader.

A good team leader will know how to encourage and motivate the team as opposed to keeping them under her thumb. People always do better when they are encouraged instead of overly criticized.

Good team leaders know how to produce results while giving the credit for those results to the rest of the team.

When you assemble a great team, they will do great things for you and for your practice. Train them well, don't micro-manage them, trust them and let them take off and do what they do best.

Once your practice gets close to $2 million gross production per year, it is time to find you a good team leader.

Your practice is now getting past the point where you can effectively manage it and still do the dentistry. Dentists often find their practice plateaus at this point because they don't have a strong team leader to run the practice.

The person that becomes a team leader has to be a special type of person. They need to have natural leadership skills, be a high achiever with attention to detail, and they need to see and understand the "big picture" when it comes to your practice and your vision for the practice.

Being the team leader is a sometimes difficult position to fill because this person is a part of your team yet they are set apart from the rest of the team due to the

authority you have given them.

They must teach, motivate and discipline the rest of the team, which keeps them somewhat isolated from really being "one of the gang" sometimes. The team leader has to understand this role and be OK with this type of a role.

This position is kind of like a high level position in a corporation where a person is hired to take the company to another level. The team leader is charged with this kind of responsibility in your practice. They will make your life easier, but the bottom line reason for their position is to take your practice to the next level. This is something everyone needs to understand.

Be careful about making the spouse of the dentist the team leader. Sometimes the team tends to view the spouse in this role as somewhat of their adversary. I know that filling this position with a spouse is a great temptation since your spouse has a very high commitment level to you and your practice, but I have rarely seen this type of situation work very well. Your spouse is also a difficult one to fire, for obvious reasons, if they are unable to accomplish what you have set before them.

Building a great incentivized team is vital to your success in creating a multi-million-dollar practice.

Your team is your greatest asset. A great team can make your life a lot easier.

A team that has a financial incentive is a powerful team that will "sell" the dentistry and keep you busy like you never have been before.

The right team will make your life so much easier and make you very wealthy.

How much should your total payroll be as a percentage of your profit and loss statement? That depends upon who you talk to. I have heard anything from 18% to 32%. My payroll runs between 25% and 30%. This is with bonus included. This is one area I don't try to cut down on because my team is my greatest asset.

My success is directly related to the quality of staff that I have and am able to attract. I treat them very well and pay them very well and I put a lot of responsibilities on them. I see trying to scrimp in that area as being dangerous to my success.

A great team is a requirement for your success. You need a team that looks to your leadership and is committed to the success of the practice. At the end of a long hard day where you had to work on the dreaded "Mrs. Jones" who is always critical of your work, never satisfied and makes you feel like you can't do anything right--you need a great team that loves you and thinks you're the greatest.

Chapter Four

Case Acceptance
Getting Patients to Say "Yes"

In talking to dentists, I find one of the most frustrating things for them is...How to get patients to do the treatment they have diagnosed? We can market our practices and bring in hundreds of new patients, but if you don't know how to get people to say "yes" to the dentistry they need, then you will never be successful.

I am always surprised that most dentists are not aware of what their "close rate" is for patients accepting their treatment recommendations. I often see close rates of around 15-20% while the doctor is guessing that it really is around 75-85%.

The reason for this discrepancy in their minds is that they don't see the patients that don't schedule. In other words, while they are presenting this complete well thought out treatment plan, the patient politely smiles and nods their head like they can't wait to get started on all the great treatment recommendations the dentist is explaining to them.

So, the dentist just assumes that the patient is running eagerly up to the front desk with opened check-book in hand, in order to pay for their full mouth rehab in advance. Why wouldn't they? - when the patient seemed just as excited as the dentist was about having this amazing transformation happen in their mouth.

After a few days go by, the dentist has forgotten about this patient, but he still has that warm fuzzy feeling inside of how this patient smiled and seemed to agree with everything that was recommended. This makes the dentist just assume that they "closed" this case when in actuality this patient almost had a heart attack at the front desk when she was handed a print out of her $27,000 treatment plan.

This dentist's team didn't say anything to him about what happened, because they don't want to hurt his feelings by telling him that he doesn't know how to present treatment effectively.

Your "close rate" is an important statistic to be aware of, and most dental software can figure this out for you.

You have probably heard some practice management consultants talk about getting 100% case acceptance. When you tell the patient what they need and give them what they want, then you have 100% case acceptance.

You give the patient the option of doing all of the treatment, some of it, or none of it. Therefore, if a patient picks "none of it", then this is still acceptance of the case because you made that offer to them as a treatment option. If a patient picks "some of it", then this is case acceptance too. There is a possibility with both of these patients that they may eventually do some or all of their needed treatment.

I understand and somewhat agree with this logic, but for me 100% case acceptance is a little bit of "smoke and mirrors".

I am interested in what my real monthly acceptance rate for dental treatment is, and what can be done to make it better. I want to know how many people that I presented treatment to, do actually wind up in the chair and have some teeth worked on.

I do agree that we should tell the patients what they need and give them what they want. I also agree that we should give the patient the options of doing all, some or none of their treatment. "None of the treatment" in my mind it really isn't case acceptance.

I think the most important thing is to change the way we do things in our practices, so it is easy for patients to say "yes" to the dental treatment they need.

This subject of case acceptance is something that we, at Quantum Leap Success in Dentistry, spend a few months working with the team and the dentist because there are so many different components that lead to success in this area. There are many specific and important steps that I am going to skip, or this book would be as thick as "War and Peace". Successful case presentation is something that you need to see and experience for you to finally "get it".

I do however want you to be able to understand the overall behavioral concepts that cause patients to say "yes" to the treatment they need. Let me start at the beginning and see if I can lay this process out for you in a way that is helpful.

**The whole process of case
acceptance by patients is much
more than what happens with
you and the patient chair-side.**

Case acceptance is counter-intuitive. In other words, what we as dentists typically think causes a patient to say "yes" to our recommendations, and what actually causes the patient to say "yes" are totally different.

Case presentation and acceptance is a huge hurdle for most dentists to change and become proficient. Again, we are back to the problem of false beliefs. I find that what most dentists believe causes patients to accept their treatment plans and what actually causes acceptance are usually two different things. How to properly do case presentations is a big one for many dentists. Some dentists will "die on this hill" even though it is costing them millions of dollars.

**Case presentation begins
with the initial new patient
phonc call to the office.**

Your front desk staff has to be trained in what to say and what not to say to a prospective new patient caller. They also have to know how to make the prospective new patient caller feel welcomed and desired, as opposed to an interruption in the fulfillment of their other front desk duties.

Unfortunately, most front desk employees see the phone as an interruption to the other things they are trying to get done, and the prospective new patient caller senses that attitude on the phone. This is especially true if you are under-staffed at the front desk.

The phone is the life blood of the practice since all new patient's first encounter with the practice is via the phone.

Yet, many dentists just hire someone for the front desk and let that person pretty much decide how they think the phone should be answered. I don't know of any other company that hires people to work their phones without giving them extensive training.

The reason why it is so important that the new patient phone call be handled properly is because the patient is going to be forming an opinion of you, the dentist, based upon how they are treated on the phone. That opinion continues by how they are treated when they walk into the practice for the first time, how they are greeted and treated by the assistant, and how they are treated by the hygienist. If any of these encounters are negative, then the patient will project that on to you.

In other words, the patient typically believes that you are like your employees, and people don't want to buy from someone they don't like.

On the other hand, if they have had a great experience with each staff member along the way before they have met you, then the impression they have in their minds is that you will be great too. It would not be congruent for the new patient to be thinking... "Wow, the staff is wonderful, helpful and friendly, but I'll bet the dentist is a jerk."

As you know, it is important that we develop a good relationship with our patients. If we, as the dentist, are busy doing dental treatment like we should be, then we must rely on the rest of the team to do most of that initial relationship building. If the patient has had a wonderful experience in the practice all along the way, then they are not necessarily expecting to have a long 30 minute to an hour one-on-one experience with the dentist.

In fact, I have found that, when this happens, the patient wonders if the dentist is any good, since he has that much time to just sit and talk.

**My patients like the fact that I
am busy, because it non-verbally
says to them that I am good
since I am in high demand.**

But, in order for this to work, you have to have a good team that understands customer service.

Remember, that the whole process we go through, starting with the initial phone call, is to make it easy for the patient to say "yes" to our treatment recommendations. Everything we do is meant to build trust and confidence that leads to treatment acceptance.

The first concept we need to understand as dentists is how most patients make decisions about whether to do treatment or not to do treatment.

**Patients make decisions about
treatment based upon emotion and
feelings, not logic and education.**

Most of us dentists are very logical and analytical. We develop our treatment plans based upon well thought out analysis and technical information.

Patients, for the most part, don't make their decisions about dental treatment that way. Now, you may get the occasional engineer that seems to make all his decisions based upon the facts alone with no emotion involved, but that is not the majority of your patients.

I still believe that even this engineer is making an emotional decision about treatment, because for these types of people a well thought out analytical approach is an emotional high for them.

Your case acceptance will go up if you have more team involvement in the process than just the dentist's involvement. This is counter-intuitive.

When the whole new patient examination process is a team approach, it gives the patient time to digest the condition of their mouth and how to tackle fixing the problems without being overwhelmed. The team will also typically be better at keeping things on an emotional level with the patient than the dentist can.

Another counter-intuitive aspect is that case acceptance actually goes up when the dentist talks less to the patient about their needed treatment, as opposed to talking a lot to try and over educate the patient.

I am not saying that the dentist should do a poor examination, but there are ways you can do a thorough examination in a shorter amount of time, with proper delegation. Having the team involved in the process helps to keep the patient from being over-whelmed with a large treatment plan. This keeps the dentist from being the only one to connect emotionally with the patient about the health of their mouth.

The things that we "sell" in dentistry are solutions to problems and good feelings.

If a patient has a cracked tooth and needs a crown, or an abscessed tooth and needs a root canal, then we are "selling" them solutions to their problems. If the patient wants cosmetic dentistry, then we are "selling" them good feelings.

If we are recommending a solution to a problem, we need to present that solution in a way that connects with the person on a feeling level, not on an intellectual level.

If we are recommending a cosmetic procedure that is "selling" good feelings, then we need to keep this on a feeling level and not clutter up the conversation with intellectual stuff like margins, types of porcelain, occlusal forces, vertical dimension, etc.

[I am putting the word "selling" in quotation marks because patients don't believe it is ethical for dentists to sell, in the context of trying to talk them into something. If a patient senses a dentist is taking this approach, they typically feel manipulated and believe their best interests are not being served. This is when they start looking for the exit signs. When I use the word "selling," I am <u>not</u> using it in the sense of trying to talk the patient into purchasing a product.]

We dentists have been taught in dental school and in CE courses that we need to thoroughly educate the patient. We have been told that we need to give them all the detailed facts and information so they can make an educated decision regarding their treatment.

The problem is that people don't make their decisions to do dental treatment based upon facts and education; they make these decisions based upon emotion. I am not advocating withholding information from the patient; we dentists just need to realize that most people don't want to know all the details. In fact, all the details actually confuse and bore them. And guess what?

Confused people don't buy.

Another thing we need to realize is that people don't want to have dental treatment done. Most patients are not all excited that they are going to get to have a crown prep done on their tooth. It is not very much fun. So, they must have an emotional reason to move them to make the decision to have a dental procedure done.

Let me give you an example that will help. Everyone knows the importance of a healthy diet and exercise for their heart health and overall health. We all know that we should limit our fat intake and keep our cholesterol at the right levels and get regular exercise. The fact is that most people don't do this even though they know intellectually all the reasons they should.

The medical community and the media have done a great job educating the public on all the facts, in order to get us to change our behavior. Yet, obesity is at an all time high in the U.S. Only 1/10th of the people that join a health club actually go.

It is obvious from this example that education doesn't change behavior. But, what if a person has a heart attack and survives? They now have a much greater likelihood of changing their behavior and eating a healthy diet and getting on a regular exercise program. Why? Because their health has now become an emotional decision due to the near death experience of a heart attack.

The educational knowledge of proper diet and exercise did not cause them to make a decision to change their behavior. An emotional event caused by a heart attack made them make a decision to change their behavior in the area of diet and exercise.

The question now is...How do we connect with the patient on an emotional level concerning their need for dental treatment?

The first advice I have for the dentist is to talk as little as possible. The longer you talk, the greater chance you have of "buying the treatment back" by moving into the analytical, intellectual part of your brain and theirs.

The second thing you need to do is to reduce your explanation of all "solutions to problems" based dental treatment to three things...

Problem – Agitation – Solution.

First, state the problem... "You have a cracked tooth". Keep this short and sweet because it doesn't take a lot of time to just state the problem. Now, what most dentists do is that they immediately go to the solution... "You need a crown". In doing this, they skipped making the emotional connection.

You have to agitate first. Agitation is telling the patient what is going to happen if they don't fix the problem. This is where you tell the patient how not fixing this problem is going to impact their life.

This is where you need to spend some time and talk about the potential for a root canal, tooth loss, pain, more expense because of more extensive treatment, etc. You can even tell them about other patients you have had, that waited and the problem got worse, more costly and painful. You have now connected with them on an emotional level.

Now, you can go to the solution after you have agitated.

Keep the solution short and sweet also... "You need a crown to strengthen the tooth". Don't go into margins, materials, amount of tooth reduction, onlays versus crowns ...you are just confusing and boring the patient. They don't want all those details. They want you to make the decision about what is best for their tooth...an onlay instead of a crown, etc.

I am not saying don't talk about different treatment options. What I am saying is don't give them a bunch of detailed information that is confusing to them and then expect them to make an informed decision. They typically trust your decision as to what the best treatment option for them is going to be. For example... "I recommend an onlay in this situation because we can strengthen the tooth and keep more tooth structure at the same time."

The patient usually just wants to know three major things.

Is it going to hurt?
How much time is it going to take?
How much is it going to cost?

How many times have you gotten the phone call on a weekend or holiday from the patient who now has a bad toothache because they didn't do the crown you recommended on the decayed and cracked tooth, with the huge amalgam sculpture? Now they have a bad tooth ache on a Saturday night and have to wait until Monday for you to do the root canal and crown.

"Agitating" the patient properly and connecting with them on an emotional level prevents these types of emergencies from happening and increases your case acceptance.

Keeping things short, and the least confusing or over-whelming to the patient, is always the best route to case acceptance. The patient's motivation for treatment is how not fixing the problem is going to cause problems for their life in general...not your great margins or gold versus non-precious metal versus full porcelain discussions.

Another thing I want to address is making your practice consumer friendly.

**We want to give patients what
they want, not try to force them
into a structured office policy that
makes our lives easier, not theirs.**

I prefer that patients enter my practice through the hygiene department, but I don't require that. If you require that, then you are losing lots of potential patients. They may be polite and schedule an appointment, but more than likely they will call another practice and no-show or cancel on your schedule.

Let me break down the new patient experience into the two ways that a patient can enter the practice because they are each treated differently. The two ways a patient can enter the practice are:

Through the hygiene department...in other words, this new patient calls and says that they want to get their teeth cleaned and checked.

On the doctor's schedule...this new patient calls and says that they have a particular problem or concern, or sometimes they just want to get their teeth checked, but don't want a cleaning.

Let's talk about how the new patient enters the practice through the hygiene department. This is the preferred way that a patient can enter the practice for several behavioral reasons.

**During the new patient's time
with the hygienist there is
more time for a relationship to
develop with the hygienist.**

The hygienist will show the patient their x-rays and intra-oral pictures of their teeth and she will spend time talking about problems that she is seeing. She will also find out about any concerns the patient has and they will spend some time talking about those. This also lets the patient feel and know that they have been heard and understood.

The hygienist will also talk to the hygiene assistant (if you use a hygiene assistant) about potential problems she is seeing and concerns she has that need to be noted on the chart, for the doctor to be sure to look at when he comes in later.

In other words, there is a dialogue going on between the hygienist, the patient, and the hygiene assistant. This gets the patient involved and it also allows the patient to hear about the condition of their mouth several times.

**It has been shown that a person
needs to hear something at least
three times in order for them to
remember, understand and "get it".**

When the dentist comes in later, the hygienist or the hygiene assistant will bring the dentist up to speed on what they have been talking about, with the patient, and any concerns that he needs to take a look at. When you state the problem, agitate and provide a solution, you are talking about what they have already been discussing prior to your coming into the room. To the patient, this feels like a second opinion.

The patient sees your hygienist and your assistant as more of a neutral second and third party. They are more open to your recommendations if this kind of dialogue has been going on before you come into the room.

The hygienist talks to the patient about possible problem areas that they are seeing; then, the hygienist tells you about the possible problems she has seen and has discussed. You then confirm the problems and what can happen as a result of these problems not getting addressed. Then, you talk about solutions to these problems. After the exam, the hygienist or hygiene assistant takes the patient up to the financial coordinator and tells her about the problems and the needed treatment recommended by the doctor.

The patient has now heard three or four times about their dental problems and the treatment they need. We have also put some urgency on doing this treatment because we have agitated and told them what could happen if they don't fix the problem(s). That same urgency has to follow through when the patient is handed off to the financial coordinator.

In other words, if the doctor has said that he is concerned about a tooth and wants to get it taken care of as soon as possible and this piece of information is not conveyed in the "hand off" from the back office to the front office, then all urgency is lost.

You don't want the team at the front desk saying to the patient... "We can get you an appointment two weeks from now."... after the doctor has said that he wants to take care of the problem in the next 2-3 days.

It is also important, when the patient is being examined by the doctor, that you let the patient know that the treatment can be done in whatever order they prefer.

What I want my patients to understand is that we can do their treatment all at once or in stages.

On a large treatment plan, this relieves the stress they may be feeling if they are thinking that we are going to try to pressure them into doing more than they are comfortable with.

As you know, sometimes treatment plans can be large, like $10,000 or $15,000 or more. In most cases, if we send a patient up to the front desk with that kind of a treatment plan, they will be over-whelmed and perhaps leave thinking that you are after their money.

The big treatment plan for patients is like trying to eat an elephant all at once. If we don't give them bite-size pieces, then they will feel overwhelmed and more often than not, do nothing or go to another office.

There are ways that I talk to the patients that will quickly set the patients' minds at ease and accomplish a few things. The first thing we don't want patients to do is to get into a conversation with us on specific fees, cost of total treatment and the myriad of insurance questions.

The second thing I don't want patients feeling is over-whelmed, so I want them to know that we will go at their pace. In other words, we can do this treatment in stages, in order of priority, or in as few appointments as possible. You have to know how to talk about this in the right way so that the patient doesn't have sticker shock at the front desk.

The third thing you don't want to happen is to have a patient at the front desk with no plan of attack and a staff member that doesn't know how to make their treatment plan affordable for them and maximize their insurance.

Our case acceptance is high because this is a well-planned process from beginning to end.

Just like a Broadway play, this has to be rehearsed and everyone has their part to play in the whole production. If not, then everyone tries to "wing it" and the result is that a patient is not getting the treatment they need because we have not made it easy for them to say "yes".

Now, let's talk about the new patient that comes into the practice on the doctor's schedule, because they have a particular concern or they are in pain.

This is typically a short appointment, but the assistant is going to do much of the same things that the hygienist did, but in a limited fashion. The assistant is going to find out what the new patient's concern is, and take x-rays. She will be dialoguing with the patient about their concern or problem and answering their questions as best she can.

When I come into the room, I am brought up to speed in front of the patient, on what is going on and what they have been talking about. This allows the patient to feel and know that they have been heard and understood.

My objective is to just focus on that one problem.

This is a limited exam, not a comprehensive one. Even if the new patient is coming in wanting a complete exam and is not having any concerns or issues, I still focus on a particular problem that I see and express my concern over that problem. I then agitate and provide a solution.

The reason I focus on one issue or concern is because the new patient's experience in hygiene is much more effective as I have previously described. Plus, there will be the periodontal evaluation with a complete probing done by the hygienist.

The new patient coming into the practice on the doctor's schedule has less of a relationship with the office and is therefore more likely to be blown away by a large complete treatment plan.

I tell the patient that, after we take care of this one area of concern, then we will get them into hygiene and measure around their gums to check for gum disease and clean off their teeth so we can see them better, to do a more thorough examination.

The assistant will be "Talking-over-the-patient" to me about their problem and concern just like the hygienist does with me and the new patient. The hand-off of the patient to the financial coordinator by the assistant is also done the same way.

One of our objectives, with this patient, is to get that dentistry done today, if at all possible. The patient likes this because they have already taken time off from work, and we like it because they are motivated to do it today and it increases our numbers for the day.

The patient is typically more motivated to do it today than they will be in the future. Also by "working in" that dentistry today you decrease the chances of the patient later changing their mind and cancelling their appointment.

Same-day-dentistry also has a much higher profitability when compared to the regularly scheduled dentistry on our appointment book. You must have the capacity and the efficiency in your systems, staff, and facility to be able to work in that same day dentistry, but this effort is well worth the increased profitability.

My favorite procedure to work in for same-day-dentistry is Lumineers. Due to their high profitability and short first appointment, they can make a tremendous jump in your daily numbers. I have had several $60,000+ days due to same-day-dentistry with Lumineers.

Let's now take a look at the cosmetic dentistry patient. I love cosmetic dentistry. My practice is <u>not</u> a spa type of cosmetic only practice, but we do quite a bit of cosmetic dentistry.

I really like Lumineers. In 2007, 2008, 2009 and so far in 2010, I have done more Lumineers than any other dentist in the world. I often have dentists ask me how we are able to do so many Lumineers. In short, it is remembering that this is an emotional decision and keeping it that way. I have Lumineers on my teeth. Half of my team has Lumineers on their teeth.

When a patient comes into the practice wanting cosmetic dentistry, they are usually "sold" before I ever see them.

The ladies in the office are showing them pictures and showing them their own Lumineers and talking about how they love their smiles. When I come in to meet the patient, a picture of their smile is on the computer monitor and I ask them how they want their smile to look different.

I look at the x-rays and look in their mouth and determine if they are a candidate for Lumineers or not. If they are, then I tell them how great they are going to look. I tell them they won't need shots or have their teeth ground down for Lumineers.

If they aren't a candidate, then I talk about their other options. The same principles apply. I don't want to overwhelm them with details they don't need to know or want to know. This is just going to confuse them. Just because you are processing this information in your mind doesn't mean that you need to verbalize all of your thoughts to the patient.

Again, I am not advocating withholding information the patient needs to make an informed decision. I am saying don't give the patient a bunch of unnecessary information that means something to you but nothing to them.

I give them their options and the pros and cons of each option; then, I get out of the room and let the team take it from there.

Just a few words on Lumineers...I know there are two camps of thought on traditional prepped veneers vs. no prep or minimal prep veneers. I did prepped porcelain veneers for most of my career: now I rarely do prepped veneers. I am one of the instructors with Den-Mat for Lumineers; so, I have not only done a lot of them, but I have also taught other dentists how to do them.

If you are not doing Lumineers, I encourage you to go take a course and do them. Lumineers are so easy to "sell" when the patient knows that in most instances they don't need a shot and don't need their teeth ground down. I know that I would not have had veneers put on my teeth if they would have had to be prepped.

If you couple the acceptance rate with the high profitability of no temporaries plus no tooth sensitivity, then, there are very few reasons for me to do prepped veneers anymore.

One of our greatest concerns is when we put porcelain veneers on someone's teeth, they will sit up and look at their smile and say they don't like them. If this happens with prepped veneers you are in deep "doo-doo" because, now what are you going to do since you took most of the enamel off their teeth?

Another factor is that Lumineers has done so much advertising, that the public knows that traditional veneers are not reversible and they are demanding no prep or minimal prep Lumineers.

Den-Mat introduced their LumiTray several months ago. As of this writing, I have done over 200 units of LumiTray cases. The seating process and the finishing process is much easier and faster than the traditional Lumineers technique.

Another great thing about the LumiTray is, if you need to do some reduction on teeth that are out of the arch form, you don't have to do that reduction until the seat appointment. Since the veneers are designed and printed by the computer, you will receive a "reduction coping" which will show you exactly where and how much tooth reduction is necessary. You reduce the teeth and put the veneers on, in that same appointment. I like the flexibility this gives me.

Now back to case presentation.

Another big component of getting patients to say "yes" is to make their treatment affordable for them, with different creative financing options.

I don't agree with in-house financing, unless it is for orthodontic treatment. Orthodontics is basically patients making payments to you for treatment that is ongoing, as opposed to restorative dentistry where the patient is making payments to you for treatment that has been completed.

You don't want patients owing you money for treatment you have completed. They will often find "problems" with your treatment, as an excuse to not pay you. Also, if they owe you money and are behind in their payments, then you now have a cancellation and no-show problem for other appointments.

We have to come up with ways to make treatment affordable for our patients. It has been determined that most people need to finance any purchase that is over $500.

The days of just asking... "Will that be cash, check or charge?"...are gone forever.

We have all been conditioned to think in terms of monthly payments. When you go to buy a car, the salesman doesn't say... "This is going to be $33,000. Will that be cash, check or charge?" Instead the salesman says... "I can get you into this beautiful car today for only $750 a month."

We need to think the same way because this is how our patients think. There are several outside financing companies today that finance dentistry, where our patients can get their treatment done not only today, but even interest free.

This is a service we need to provide in our practices because most of the time patients will not take the initiative on their own to figure out how they are going to pay for treatment. They want you to figure it out for them. They want you to tell them how you can get their monthly payment to a number they can afford.

You need a sharp, motivated and properly trained front desk staff to make this work effectively.

In getting high case acceptance, just remember that the more you say, the greater chance you are going to talk the patient out of treatment. Our job is not to educate the patient into an intellectual decision.

Our job is to connect with them on an emotional level by telling them and showing them how not fixing the problem is going to negatively impact their life.

Again, I am not advocating withholding necessary information and options that a patient needs to consider. I am saying that in my experience many dentists talk way too much with their patients about technical information that the patient does not need to know, nor so they understand. Most of the time, they will smile and nod their heads all the while thinking to themselves that they have no idea what you are talking about.

Remember a confused patient doesn't buy. Also, remember that your staff will probably be much better at "selling" treatment to your patients than you are. Our brains have been contaminated with too much technical and analytical stuff from dental school.

The sooner you as the dentist can get out of the way, the sooner your team will get them scheduled to do the work. But, your team has to be well trained and incentivized to do so.

There are many, many other details in the whole process of case presentation that lead to a "yes" by the patient. It is not possible for me to cover all of these details in this book, mainly because most of these strategies have to be seen and experienced by you and your team. This will cause case presentation to make sense and come together in your mind and your team's mind.

One of the things the dentists and their teams in our consulting program receive are DVD's actually showing us, with patients, doing what we are teaching. Our Platinum Plus level clients and staff also get to come and spend a day in my office while we are seeing patients. This is really the only way to learn effective case presentation from start to finish.

This should give you an overview though, of how we get patients to say "yes" to the dental treatment they need, which of course is a requirement to building the multi-million-dollar practice.

Again, everything we do in the practice is done to make it easy for a patient to say "yes" to the treatment they need. A high close-rate on your case acceptance is a well orchestrated chain of events and experiences by the patient with you and your office staff, to make it easy for them to say "yes".

You don't want to hear the dreaded phrase... "I'll think about it"...which usually means that you failed to connect with them on an emotional level, to create urgency and find a way to make it affordable for them.

Chapter Five

Scheduling For Maximum Profitability

Your schedule controls the productivity of your practice. There are only so many hours in the day and each of those hours has a certain value, based upon your level of production.

Therefore, the ladies, in your office that control your schedule, also control how much you can and will produce. Whoever you allow to schedule appointments has a very important job with a lot of responsibility. This person or persons need to know how to schedule for maximum profitability.

I like to keep things simple and as uncomplicated as possible. Many of the things we do in the dental office can be greatly simplified and made much more efficient. I give this preface because there are a lot of different scheduling techniques being taught that, in my opinion, are so complicated it just makes life difficult for your team at the front desk.

For instance, you can schedule each procedure with assistant time, then doctor time followed by assistant time and finally even clean-up-the-room time. You can also block out time on the schedule for specific procedures for specific times of the day and for specific days of the week.

There is also "perfect day" scheduling where the person scheduling tries to put in certain types of procedures at certain times on certain days so that once in a blue moon you can say that you had a "perfect day".

A perfect day for me is one where we did more in production than our daily goal was. Another "perfect day" is the day that the dreaded "Mrs. Jones", who just the thought of makes sweat bead up on your brow, is NOT on the schedule.

For me, these different scheduling methods are trying to organize and schedule things that can not always be scheduled.

In other words, we are trying to schedule people that are sometimes late; sometimes spend ten minutes in the restroom; decide they want to see their account history for the last 5 years; decided they want to do two crowns and one filling instead of two fillings and one crown; or you start on their tooth and there is decay into the pulp and now you are adding a root canal in with the crown you planned; etc.

No matter how hard we try, it is almost impossible to get all the doctor times in one column of the schedule to line up perfectly with the assistant times in the next column and vice-versa. Also, the "perfect day" rarely happens and if it does...so what?

My team and I all work together to make the schedule all come together, and it rarely happens like we had it scheduled at the beginning of the day. We have all the "same day dentistry" we add into the schedule and all the other changes that invariably happen.

To build a multi-million-dollar practice, you have to know how to build flexibility into your schedule for maximum daily profitability.

Trying to schedule all of this perfectly is trying to make something ordered out of something that is a little chaotic by its very nature. You have to be comfortable with the fact that, to have maximum daily profitability, you have to realize that the schedule is a living thing that is constantly evolving.

You and your team have to know how to work together as a well-oiled machine to make the necessary changes and problem-solve during the day to make the schedule work. If you or your team view emergencies and adding "same day dentistry" to the schedule as an inconvenience, then you are sabotaging your success.

I love "same day dentistry" for several reasons. The patient is more motivated to do their dentistry today. If you diagnose the treatment today and appoint the patient to do it next week, then you increase the risk that the patient will change their mind.

They might talk to their co-worker and get talked into going to their dentist for a second opinion. They could get nervous about having the procedure done and decide to wait. They could turn on the TV and the talking heads tell them how afraid they should be about the recession and economic problems.

They could talk to their sister-in-law's niece on the phone, who used to be a dental assistant 7 years ago, and has the "expertise" to diagnose over the phone and convince the patient that your diagnosis is wrong.

Patients also love to have their treatment done today because they are already there and don't have to take off work again.

The key to making "same day dentistry" work on your schedule is to have capacity in both treatment rooms and staff and systems to make adjustments to get the job done.

It is kind of like the quarter-back of a football team making an audible play change at the line of scrimmage because the defensive line changed to a different formation. For this to work, the rest of the offensive line has to understand what the audible play call means and know what to do as a result of the play change. This is what your team learns to do with a busy schedule.

I typically use three assistants and three treatment rooms. I have another room ready to go and an assistant for that room, if necessary. I have two rooms that are scheduled for production primarily, and another room is scheduled for seating lab cases, emergencies, adjustments and new patients coming in for a limited exam.

My front desk knows the total times to schedule for different types of procedures and they stagger them from one room to the next. Most appointments require only a small percentage of the time for the doctor; therefore by staggering the appointments in the three rooms, I am able to go from room to room and maximize my profitability.

The first appointment of the day we schedule differently.

At the start of the day we have three rooms all scheduled at 8:00 am.

I know this looks impossible because I can't be in three places at once, but it always works out. The reasons are that Mrs. Jones is going to want to finish her coffee, and Mrs. Smith is ten minutes late and so on. We put them all in at 8:00 and it always works out.

One problem that I see most dentists make is that they staff their practice for the slow times of the day, not the busy times of the day.

This causes a capacity problem that greatly reduces your ability to reach maximum profitability. Don't think that you are over-staffed because you have an assistant with no patient during the middle of the day. You are losing money in lost production if you can't add in same day dentistry during the busy parts of the day.

Patients want to come to our office when it is convenient for them, not when it is convenient for us. You will pay for that assistant's salary many times over each month by having another room in which you can schedule production.

You don't make anything sitting at your desk because there is no assistant to take care of those extra patients that could be added to your schedule during the busy times of the day.

This is of course assuming that you have the capacity with an additional treatment room. If you equip another treatment room it will cost you about $30 a day. You will need an assistant in that treatment room which will cost you another $200 per day. So, you total cost for another treatment room will be around $250 per day.

If you average adding in only one crown and build-up per day then you can see what a great profit margin you will have. We typically add in $5000 to $10,000+ per day in same-day-dentistry.

When you have a well trained team, everything just works out. They are all working to find a way for everything to work in real time. Making the schedule work is the team's responsibility, not mine. I don't decide where a patient is scheduled or how to change things or move things to get the schedule to work. The team takes care of this and they can do it far better than I ever could.

My job is to focus on the patient and taking care of them and not deciding where, if and how we are going to work in some "same day dentistry".

All of my team wear the little radio ear pieces so that they are constantly communicating with each other. I do not wear one. I just wait for them to tell me which room to go to next and, when I get there, I find out what I will be doing.

When I walk into the room, the assistant tells me, or points to the chart, or has written down what we are doing and I get to work. I don't want to think about the schedule, I just want to think about the patient. The team keeps me on time and makes sure that the schedule works.

The point of all this is to make everything extremely efficient. The more efficient I am and the team is, then the more dentistry I am able to do. My stress level is also lower because I am not worrying about everything else that is going on in the office.

But, in order to do this, you as the dentist have to give up control and trust your staff to do what they do. If they do not have an incentive, with a bonus system, then it stands to reason that they are not going to be that motivated to take on this added responsibility.

The team also comes to learn pretty quickly that the harder they work you, then the more money they make. They soon realize that you increase their income when you are sitting in your chair in the treatment room, not when you are sitting in your chair in your office. You then get to do what you like to do most which is work on teeth, and leave all that other stuff to your team.

If you are a micro-manager and a little OCD, then you will need to change this about yourself or your staff will never be able to take wing and fly with this model. I regularly do $30,000 and $40,000 days with this approach to scheduling. Do you want this level of production bad enough to change? This will be one of those false belief areas you will need to get in touch with and change, or it will cost you a lot in lost production and collections.

One thing you really want to watch out for on your schedule is too much scheduled time for procedures.

For instance, you don't want to see one hour blocks of time scheduled for seating one crown. Your profitability on that crown just went way down. If it takes a long time to seat a crown, then you need to have a talk with your lab.

If you are seeing a patient and then sitting at your desk for 15 minutes, then going to see another patient and going back to your desk for 20 minutes, then you are not being scheduled effectively, or you need more patients.

You also need to be working on your speed if it is taking you too long to do a procedure. Are there things you are doing that can be delegated to your staff? Make sure that your assistants are doing everything they can legally do. My practice is in Texas which has no expanded duties for assistants or hygienists, yet we are still able to make things work by delegating the things I can legally delegate.

Take a close look at how you spend your time during the day.

Figure out what your time is worth per minute.

Take your monthly production and divide it by the number of days you work in a month. Now divide that by the number of hours in your day. Now divide that by 60 and see what your time is worth per minute. You will be surprised at how much your time is worth.

My time is worth around $25 per minute at my level of production, so, guess what it costs me to make the temporary crown instead of the assistant? What does it cost me if I use an auto cure product instead of a light cure product? What does it cost me if I like to tell lots of jokes to the patients every day?

There is nothing wrong with these things as long as you know what it is costing you and you are OK with that. Another way to look at the value of your time is...How much more can I make if I learn how to cut a crown prep faster? How much more profitable can I be with a procedure, if I use faster materials? How much more profitable can I be if I use the H&H cordless impression technique? This is all becoming better at the business of dentistry, because your dental practice is a business.

Another thing that is really important with your schedule is to look at how long people have to wait to get on the doctor's schedule or the hygiene schedule.

If new patients have to wait two weeks or longer to get on to the hygiene schedule, then you are losing patients. People will typically not wait over two weeks to get in. This is the age of convenience. We want convenience and we want it now.

If patients have to wait two weeks or more, they will often times go ahead and make an appointment on your hygienist's schedule and then call other offices to try to find a more convenient time. They will then either cancel or no-show on you. If you are having this problem, you need to increase your hygiene capacity by adding a part-time hygienist and/or hiring a hygiene assistant.

I prefer using a hygiene assistant for my existing hygienist before hiring another hygienist because it is always easier to work with the hygienist you already have than break in a new one. A hygiene assistant will make your hygienist about twice as productive as she is by herself.

Take a look at your hygiene schedule and see how full it is two weeks out. If it is pretty full, then you have a capacity problem which is limiting the number of new patients you can see.

This is also a problem for getting scaling and root planing procedures booked into hygiene. Your cancellation and no-show rate will go way up on these procedures when you book them out that far. The urgency in the patient's mind goes down and the broken appointment and cancellation rate goes way up.

Realize that your schedule controls your income level. We either get in control of our schedule or it controls us. If your team is not incentivized with a good bonus system, then they will want to keep the schedule light because it is less hectic for them. If you give them an incentive and empower them to run the schedule, they will work your buns off!

Chapter Six

Marketing Your Practice

Times have changed drastically in dentistry over the last several years. Now, more than ever, people make their decisions on what dentist to go to, from marketing. I think that we can all agree that referred patients are the best new patients because they usually come to us with a level of relationship and trust that is higher than the marketing generated new patient. The referred patient also costs us a lot less than the marketing generated patient.

As the individuals in our society become more and more isolated and independent, we have seen a decrease in the referral rate, compared to years past. Many people these days don't even know their next door neighbor, after living next to them for years.

We have a monthly new patient referral rate at around 50% of all of our new patients. Referrals are important to us and we greatly value them, but we cannot get the number of patients we need to continue to grow from referrals alone. However, the more we market, the more referrals we see.

There are very specific things you can do in your practice to increase your referral rate. If you do absolutely nothing to stimulate referrals in your practice, you will normally get 15-20% referrals. This is the rate that people will refer to a dental office, without having any incentive or encouragement from within the office to do so.

We give an incentive to our patients so that they will refer people to us, which works very well to keep the referral numbers up.

External marketing is a necessity for the multimillion-dollar practice. You have to get more than your fair share of new patients and take advantage of other dentist's inability or unwillingness to market their practices.

We do lots of different kinds of external marketing. We do direct mail, radio, local magazines, newsletters, website, newspaper inserts and yellow pages. I believe that the yellow pages are quickly becoming a thing of the past. We still have a fairly good return on investment on the yellow pages, but it continues to drop from year to year, as more people make the shift to the internet.

When you look at marketing your dental practice, there are a couple of different ways that you can approach it. One way is to put out an ad that basically conveys to the public... "here I am, this is my name, these are all the organizations I am a member of, I am the greatest dentist around so you would be an idiot not to come to me." In other words, this ad (which is the type of ads most dentists run) is basically telling the public how wonderful you and your office are, and that they should come to your office because you are so fantastic.

My problem with these advertisements is that they do not answer the question that we all have as human beings....
"What is in it for me?"

Most people don't care how great you are as a dentist, they just expect that. When you read an advertisement, the features and benefits of the office should <u>not</u> be able to be followed with the statement... *"Well, I should hope so!"* For example: **"Gentle Dentistry"** can be followed with the statement... *"Well, I should hope so!"* Here is another:

"We care about you."... *"Well, I should hope so!"* **"Doctor takes a lot of continuing education"**... *"Well, I should hope so!"* In other words, many of dental office advertising states benefits that the patient expects as <u>normal</u> in any dental office, and the dentist thinks it is a big deal.

How about this for a benefit? **"24 months interest-free financing."** That <u>can't</u> be followed with... *"Well, I should hope so!"* How about? **"Free Exam, X-rays and Consultation"** – or – **"Free Teeth Whitening"**. That <u>can't</u> be followed with... *"Well, I should hope so!"* All of these benefits also answer the question in the patient's mind of... *"What is in it for me?"*

The point of your advertising is to make it very easy for people to call you and make an appointment.

The goal is to take away as much, if not all, of the risk for them to come to see you. We have to change because society has changed. We all want things done as quickly and conveniently as possible.

Most people are not willing to wait in line to come to see you. They don't care that you like every Wednesday and Friday off, if they want to come in on a Wednesday or a Friday. A multi-million-dollar practice has to become consumer friendly. The days, of getting patients to fit into our hours and our policies and our systems, that are designed for our convenience and not the patients, are quickly coming to a close.

When you have a multi-million-dollar practice, you need to get more than your fair share of patients in your community. Therefore, you need to remove as many barriers and road blocks to new patients coming to your office, as possible; and give the public lots of reasons why they should come to you instead of anyone else.

Most all of the forms of advertising mediums work...direct mail, newspaper, newsletters, radio, TV, yellow pages, internet, etc. The secret is not which medium of advertising to use, but the type of advertising you are doing in that medium.

Many times I will hear a doctor say..."I tried that direct mail (or radio, or newspaper, etc.) and it doesn't work in my area." You need to realize that the different mediums of advertising work. What causes the ad not to work is the design of the ad, not the medium. You have to know how to design an ad that will get a response from the public.

In my marketing my purpose is to remove all the risk and all the barriers I can to get a person to come try our office out and see if we are the right place for them. One of the ways I do this is to give a free exam, x-rays and consultation to the new patient.

Sometimes dentists tell me...
"But, look how much money we are losing by giving away all those exams and x-rays!"

My response is... *"Look how much dentistry I get to do because I give these away free."* Back when I was a money-poor dentist, I refused to give away my exams and x-rays free. After all, I thought that the patient needed to pay for and value my time and expertise.

I now believe that most of my patients value my time and expertise even when I give them a free exam and free x-rays. There are some that don't, but they typically don't value anyone else's time either; so, I don't get my feelings hurt.

I know that I have stepped on some toes because I used to be there too. The dynamics of a multimillion-dollar practice are different when it comes to marketing and consumerism.

For me, it came down to the fact that I would rather have a multi-million-dollar dental practice by catering to the consumer and making it easier for lots of people to come to see me.

As opposed to trying to project the image that I am the "greatest-dentist-in-the-land" and that the patients should feel privileged to come to see me. The last approach does appeal to a segment of the market, but it is a very small segment, which I believe is getting smaller every year.

You need to make marketing your dental practice a regular expense, just like your lab bill and dental supplies. Most dentists advertise when things get slow...which is too late...and then they stop advertising when things pick up...which makes things get slow again. You can level out your new patient flow by setting aside 3-6% of your P&L for marketing and do it every month, like clock-work.

We never know how well a marketing piece is going to do until we put it out there and see. It typically takes 3-6 months to evaluate a piece of marketing, to see if it has a good return on investment. You may have spent several thousands of dollars and six months time to find out that the marketing piece didn't work very well.

It is very beneficial if you can copy a piece of marketing that has already been shown to be successful by another dentist, who is not in your area of course. This has been a major benefit to our clients in Quantum Leap Success in Dentistry.

We have marketing pieces that have been proven to work in my practice, which our clients get to use.

We are also able to do the design, printing and mailing of direct mail pieces for our Platinum Plus clients, <u>at our cost,</u> and the Gold and Silver clients receive a discount on their direct mail cost. This saves them thousands of dollars every month.

One more important item about marketing...

When you spend money on marketing, you are <u>not</u> paying for new patients. You are only paying to get your phone to ring.

A patient that calls your practice, due to your marketing, is not as easy to schedule as a referred patient. They have nothing at stake and they have no relationship with you at all. Your front desk staff has to be well trained on how to convert this caller into a new patient. This does not come naturally to the people at the front desk, so you will just be throwing your advertising dollars away if they are not properly trained on answering the phone.

This is very costly because you are not only losing what it costs you to advertise that phone to ring, but you have lost the dentistry

that you would have done.

You will never know what you have lost because you don't know how many patients the front desk staff is losing on the phone. People will just say... *"I'll check my schedule and call you back."* Translated, this really means... *"I am going to call another office because you never drew me in and made me excited about your office, nor did you even ask me if I wanted to make an appointment."*

With our Platinum Plus and Gold level clients we do recorded "new patient" audit calls to their practices on a regular basis. This allows the doctor, and staff person taking the call, to hear how they are handling the phone call of the prospective new patient. This feedback is very valuable to the staff person who is learning how to improve their phone skills. This recording is also valuable to the doctor to hear how his front desk staff are really handling the phone call of the potential new patients.

Marketing can also accentuate the problems in your office. If you are having capacity problems and your new patient flow goes from 25 per month to 75 per month, then your problem just got three times worse. Marketing is not always the *immediate* solution to a slow practice. As I said earlier in this book, get some help from a dental coach or consultant.

Don't try this at home by yourself. You can make your life worse, not better.

There are consultants in the dental field, that believe my approach, to practicing dentistry, is reducing dentistry to a commodity where people view all dentistry as the same and therefore make their decision on price alone.

Yes, there are some patients who have this mentality. You know them...they are the shoppers that seem to care only about cost. I believe these people are this way about everything in their lives, not just dentistry.

I do attract this type of patient when I market my practice with offers that are designed to make it easy for people to come to my practice and try us out. These types of patients are a small percentage of the total number of patients that my marketing brings in, since I believe that these types of people are a small percentage of the population in general.

I believe that it is the old 80/20 rule. There may be 10% to 20% of the people that respond to your marketing, that you don't want in your practice. These people are such a pain in the "you know what" that they stand out in our minds, so we often think that there are more of them than the "good" patients. I believe that they are only 10-20% of the patients that come in with the marketing we do, because they are only 10-20% of the population in general.

Most of the patients that respond to my marketing don't see dentistry as a commodity and don't consider dentists and dentistry to all be the same.

They realize that there is "good dentistry" and "bad dentistry", and they, of course, want the good dentistry.

They expect me to be good at what I do, and they expect convenience, and they expect the cost of their treatment to be at a fair fee, and they like us to make it easy for them to come to see us. The consumer of today expects and demands a lot, and, in my opinion, the dentists, that meet those demands, will prosper in the future and those that don't will not. In my mind, that has nothing to do with dentistry as a commodity.

There are also some that say by marketing with offers I am trying to compete on price. I disagree. First of all, I keep my fees in the 80th percentile, so offering a discount on the exams and x-rays does not mean that I am trying to compete on price. My purpose is to remove as many barriers as possible so that the new patient will come to my practice; and also to reduce any risks on their part so as to encourage a potential patient to call my office instead of the other 100 dentists in my area.

With my marketing I am taking all of the risk for the patient and removing as many "hurdles" as possible they may have to overcome to try out my office.

The type of external marketing that I do helps to build a practice that is recession proof.

I think it is very scary, in this economy, to try to build a practice that is based on a high fee, low patient flow and a high case average type practice model.

I guess we would all like to only see two patients a day, work three days a week and produce $400K per month. I just don't think that is realistic, or even possible especially in today's economy.

I have found out that most of the consultants, promoting the building of this kind of practice, are not dentists. I do think that it is possible to build this kind of practice, but it has been my observation that most dentists are not able to make this model work. I tried to make this type of practice work for years, and after almost 19 years of barely making ends meet, I gave up on it.

Those types of practices are seeing a huge slow down as patients are worried in this slow economy, and start holding onto their wallets with both hands.

As I write the second edition of this book in June 2010, my numbers are still increasing, even though we are seeing some of the worst economic problems since the Great Depression.

I finished 2009 at $4.2 million in collections, and am on track to finish 2010 at around $5 million+. I have noticed that the recession has affected our practice. What it has done is made us aware that we really must be on top of our game; but, our philosophy of practice, our systems and our great team keep us from experiencing the slowdown like many other dentists are experiencing.

I have always structured my practice where the large cases are the icing on the cake, but not the cake itself.

I am still netting over a million dollars a year even though some economists say that we have been in a recession since December 2007. It sure makes more sense to me to build a multi-million-dollar practice that has a marketing model that will thrive in any economy. In fact, my marketing becomes more effective in this kind of economy, especially since many dentists hunker down and cut marketing expenses as the economy slows.

External marketing of your practice in the right way is a necessity in building a multi-million-dollar practice, especially in today's economy.

Chapter Seven

The Need For Systems

How many times have you tried to implement something new in your practice? It may have been a new way to better care for your patients, like taking every patient's picture and putting it in their chart so the team would recognize them when they walk in the door. It may have been asking each satisfied patient for a referral and giving them business cards. It may have been asking patients for their testimonial when they say something positive about their experience at your office.

We have all had these great ideas, so we have a staff meeting and tell the team what we are going to start doing. We all talk about the benefits to us and to the patients. We all talk about the steps of implementing this new thing and everyone agrees to start doing it tomorrow.

One month later, you realize that your team stopped doing this new thing two weeks ago! So, you have another team meeting and ask everyone what happened. Why isn't everyone doing what everyone agreed they would do? The team then agrees they will follow through this time. You feel really good that everything got sorted out and now everyone is going to start doing the new thing!

You forget about the new thing because you assume it is being done. Two months later you begin to notice that the new thing is not being done. In fact, you look into it a little deeper and you find out that the team hasn't done the new thing for 6 weeks! It is at this time that you pretty much give up on the new thing. You tell yourself that maybe it wasn't all that good of an idea anyway.

What your team is doing is just human nature. All of us revert back to doing the things that are most comfortable and the easiest for us to do.

This is why we need systems for everything we do in our offices. These systems need to be written down and taught to the team. When we have written systems, then we can hold people accountable for wavering from the agreed upon system.

Your systems are always changing. We are always tweaking them and making them more efficient, or adding new systems. If you don't have specific systems in your practice, you may notice that your practice starts to evolve into something that you may not like.

What is happening is: in the absence of clear direction from systems, your team is forced to come up with their own way of doing things.

This evolves the practice into what they think works best. This may not be in line with your desires and your vision for the practice.

As you add new employees, the way your practice operates and the vision of what you want it to look like gets further and further diluted. This is because the new employees come into your practice and do things the way they used to do them at their previous office, which is probably not at all in line with the way you want things done.

In a large practice, you can see how not having clearly defined systems can cause real chaos. This is another reason why multi-million-dollar practices need a strong team leader to oversee things and make sure that the systems are being followed. You need to be doing the dentistry and not trying to monitor this.

You are also usually the last one to realize that a particular system is not being followed because you have loupes on your face and a hand-piece in your hand.

The system at the front, that is not being followed, is the last thing on your mind, and you are in the treatment room, not up front, so you have no idea that they stopped doing that part of the system months ago. A good coach and consultant will fix that for you.

With our Quantum Leap Success In Dentistry clients, we have their teams trained in our systems, that have been proven to work. We have systems, for every area of the practice, that get the dentistry scheduled, paid for and completed. Systems keep things running smoothly, efficiently and profitably.

You need a system for every single area of your practice. Systems keep things from falling through the cracks. Systems make everything in your practice operate a peak efficiency and this translates to peak profitability. Systems improve your patient care that you are able to deliver. The right systems are critical to the success of your practice.

Numbers You Should Measure

There are many different numbers in our practices that we can measure. There are production, collections, number of new patients, number of referrals, percentage of referrals, case acceptance percentage, case average, accounts receivables, profit and loss statement percentages, balance sheet, profitability, overhead, doctor's time value per hour or minute, percentage of patients in recall, return on investment for marketing, etc. We can drive ourselves crazy trying to keep track of all of these numbers, so it is important to know which ones we need to track and how often. We also need to know if the numbers are good or if they are getting out of balance?

**In Quantum Leap we monitor
our doctors' numbers because they
give us valuable information for the
continued health of the practice.**

Different practice management speakers and consultants all have their favorite numbers to watch and measure. I will tell you the numbers that I watch and measure closely.

**It is very important to measure
your numbers, because whatever
you measure will increase.**

I will periodically look at most of my different numbers and ratios, but there are some statistics on my practice that I watch constantly because I consider them to be the most vital.

Here are my favorite statistics to measure and monitor closely.

New Patients – This is of course the life blood of your practice. We all need a steady and growing supply of new patients. This number also reflects the success of our external marketing campaigns. From this number, I also want to know the number of new patients that are referrals. You really need at least 40% of your total monthly new patients in referrals. I monitor my number of new patients on a daily basis and especially on a monthly basis.

Case Average – This number is calculated by dividing the number of new patients you saw in a month into the total production for that month. You can also figure this for a quarter of a year or for a year. This number is more of a benchmark figure than an exact number since you have hygiene production and treatment done on existing patients, included in this number. But, it is a number that will quickly tell you a lot about the health of your practice.

Your case average will give you a good handle on how well you are doing on your case acceptance.

A good healthy number for a general practice is around a $2000 - $3000 case average per new patient.

If your case average goes way below this number, then you probably have a problem in either the patients not scheduling for the treatment you recommend, or you are not diagnosing or recommending all the treatment that needs to be done.

Larger practices that are seeing over 120 new patients per month will typically have a lower case average of around $1500 to $1800. There are some things you can do to keep this case average from going down, with a larger practice that I have discovered.

**My practice presently sees around
150 new patients per month and
we maintain a $2000 to $3000
case average per month.**

Practices that do a lot of higher cost procedures like implants, full mouth re-constructions or spa cosmetic practices will typically have a higher than normal case average. These practices also typically have problems with huge fluctuations in their monthly production and they are usually the first to be hit hard in a down economy.

**One thing you want to watch for
is having a high case average and
a low number of new patients.**

This can mean that you are "over-selling" patients. This will be reflected in a low new patient referral number. In other words, a few of the patients do the recommended treatment but they are reluctant to refer their family and friends because it costs them so much to get their teeth fixed.

I talked to a dentist once that was only seeing 7-10 new patients a month but the case average was around $7500 per new patient. This dentist had almost no referrals. What was happening was that most all amalgams were being replaced with in office CAD/CAM porcelain restorations. This may be the best and finest dentistry that can be done for patients, but it is not necessarily the best thing to do if you are trying to build a healthy multi-million-dollar practice.

Another really helpful thing you can learn from your case average is how many new patients you will need each month to reach your production goals.

For instance, if you have a $2000 new patient case average and your monthly production goal is $150,000 per month, then you will need 75 new patients per month. If you work 16 days in a month, then you are going to need to see around 5 new patients per day and produce $9,375 per day.

Production/Collections – These are numbers you should track on a daily basis. I think all dentists track these numbers. You need to break out your hygiene department production and collections and let your hygienist be aware of that number. Remember, what you measure will increase. If your hygienists are on commission, you can be sure that they will be monitoring these numbers.

One of the things to monitor is the ratio of production to collections, in order to get an idea of how well you are collecting what you produce.

In my opinion, your collections should be 98 to 100 percent of your production each month.

This leads us into talking about your A/R.

Accounts Receivables – Some consultants advocate that your total A/R (30, 60 and 90 days) should not exceed 1.5 times or 150% of your monthly production. This would mean that, if you are producing $100,000 per month, then the total A/R should not be more than $150,000. <u>I do not agree that this is a healthy number.</u>

High A/R numbers, especially in 60 or 90 days, mean that either you are doing in-house financing, or you do a lot of orthodontics with payment plans, or you have a lot of past due insurance claims that are not being collected, or you have loose financial arrangements that are causing a collection problem.

In my practice, our A/R stays around 10 - 20% of my collections, which is a number that I feel more comfortable with.

I have tight financial arrangements with my patients. By this I mean that they are very clear about what it is going to cost them and how they are going to pay for it and when that amount will be due. We get all of their "out-of-pocket" costs either up front or at the time of treatment. We don't do any in-house financing but we do a whole lot of outside financing with various companies.

I also have a wonderful team member who stays up on collecting any past due accounts, which are typically from slow paying insurance companies. You need to do electronic filing of insurance claims because this eliminates the "we never got the claim" stall tactic that insurance companies use. You then need to stay on the insurance companies for payment of claims over thirty days out. When you do this, you will get a reputation with the insurance companies of not playing their games. This goes a long way in getting your claims paid on time.

A high A/R is usually a good indication that your financial arrangements with patients need to be tightened up and cleaned up.

Profit and Loss Statement – A P&L needs to be organized in a way that is more meaningful and helpful to you than your accountant. When your accountant looks at your P&L, he is looking for things that are important for your taxes but are not necessarily that helpful for you in knowing the health of your practice. Talk with your accountant about reorganizing your P&L into just the six categories below.

It takes me about 5 minutes to look at my P&L every month and get a good idea of how my practice is doing.

I have broken my P&L down into categories that are important to me in monitoring the profit of my practice. In these categories, I am more interested in knowing what I spent as a percentage of income than I am in knowing what the actual number was.

These are the categories and the percentage ranges that I break down all my different expenditures into.

Marketing	3	-	6%
Payroll	25	-	30%
Facility	7	-	9%
Dental Supplies	5	-	7%
Office Supplies	2	-	2%
Lab Expense	8	-	10%
Total Overhead	50	-	64%

By simplifying your P&L into these categories, then you can quickly look each month at your percentages and see if anything is out of line. For instance, if your dental supplies are running 9-10%, then your dental assistants are probably warehousing supplies instead of letting your supply company do that. If your lab expense is 12-14%, then you may need to negotiate lower lab fees with your dental lab. If your payroll percentage is 18-22%, then you may have a capacity blockage and need to hire another employee to be able to grow to the next level.

Remember, that the best and easiest way to reduce your overhead is to increase your production and collections. Put most of your effort in growing your practice instead of trying to cut costs.

Multi-million-dollar practices typically have higher percentages of overhead than do smaller practices, which may be at the 64 % mark on the P&L. I don't get too worried about this. Would you rather make 36% of a $4 million dollar practice or 50% of a $1 million dollar practice? That's a pretty easy question to answer for me!

Has it ever frustrated you to look at the bottom of the P&L and see a nice fat number called "net income" or "retained earnings", yet that money is nowhere to be found?

The thing to realize about your P&L, is that principal of your note payments show up on your balance sheet, not on your P&L. This is why you show "net income" at the bottom of your P&L, yet that money is nowhere to be found. Those funds went to make your note payments. Be sure to add your note payments by hand back into your P&L in the appropriate category, so you can get an accurate idea of what your profit is in real dollars.

Return on Investment (ROI) for marketing – These are very important numbers to evaluate your various types of marketing. If your ROI is low, like less than 4:1 or 5:1, then you may need to re-evaluate if those marketing dollars would be better spent on some different marketing that has a better ROI.

Most software programs have the ability to track these numbers. In order for these numbers to be accurate and make any sense, your front desk team has to be trained to ask every patient how they found out about your office and then record that information in the computer.

> **If you can't measure your marketing ROI, then you may be wasting a lot of money because you have no way of knowing which marketing is working and which marketing is not.**

By measuring your marketing, you can also make changes to a marketing campaign, in order to measure which offer or style has the best draw.

I know that I have just given you a simplistic look at what can be a complex issue. Some doctors have gotten themselves into difficult situations with high equipment and facility costs and high debt, to where there is not enough production to cover that expense. Then, there are not enough funds left for marketing, to bring in the needed new patients, so they find themselves in "catch 22". Situations like this need a consultant to help figure out a plan of attack to help them get this situation turned around as quickly as possible.

Chapter Nine

Recession Proof Your Practice

As everyone is well aware, we have just had the largest stock market drop, the largest banking crisis, the largest mortgage crisis, resulting in the largest worldwide financial crisis since the Great Depression. No one knows when, or if, the economy will recover to where we once were.

One of the great things about dentistry is that our profession, by its nature, is more recession proof than most other industries. That is not to say that we aren't affected.

There are some specific things we can do with our practices to make them recession proof.

I see all kinds of consultants and guru's today advertising how they have the solution to make your practice recession proof. I am sure that they have some answers, but I believe that some of it is probably just sales hype.

I do know from experience that you can do some things that will help keep your numbers from going down and, in fact, make your practice more recession proof, because I am presently doing that in my practice.

If you have a practice that offers a lot of different services for your patient, then you will have a practice that is more recession proof than the dentist with a spa cosmetic practice or a "big case" practice. I think that is pretty obvious.

What I have found is, as the economy gets tougher, the problems in your practice become exaggerated. For example, a poor case acceptance problem gets even worse because in a down economy it becomes harder to sell the dentistry.

The poor phone skills of the front desk team become more obvious because there are less new patients calling, so you really start feeling their low conversion rate of getting new patients on the schedule. Or, the dentist's and the team's inability to create urgency in the patients mind, for treatment on an emotional level, lead to the patient doing their fillings but not their crowns.

In a recession, your game has to come up a few notches in all the different aspects of your practice, if you want to continue to grow or even survive. You can grow and prosper in a recession but your game has to be better than it ever was. Your game has to be better than the other dentists in your area too.

I am still making my goals and growing my practice in this down economy because I know the "50 secrets" and how to get them to all work synergistically together.

Even in this economy I am still netting over $1,000,000 a year in my practice. I have done that over the last five years and I will do that again in 2010. You can to if that is what you want.

I have actually chosen not to participate in this economic down turn. You have got to stop listening to all of the "talking heads" on TV telling you how bad things are. I am not saying to "stick your head in the sand", but you can make the decision that you will prosper in this economy instead of "hunkering down" and hoping it will one day blow over.

If you do not make the right changes then you will wake up one day and have to try and catch up with the success that passed you by. We live in a different world today than even a year ago. What used to work in your practice won't work anymore. Those who make the necessary changes will prosper.

If you look throughout history, anytime there were major shifts in the economy, manufacturing, culture, technology, business, etc., those who saw the changes and made the necessary adjustments not only survived but prospered.

There were thousands of millionaires made during the industrial revolution. There were thousands of millionaires made during the Great Depression. There were thousands of millionaires made during the huge shift in technology with the computer age. There were thousands of millionaires made in the "dot com" stock market collapse a few years ago. There are also thousands of millionaires being made in this present economic downturn.

There is a polarization that happens during these paradigm shifts in history. There are those who see the changes and take the necessary steps to capitalize on those changes. There are also those that see the changes, bury their heads and hope "things get back to normal". You cannot continue to practice like you always have and prosper in this new economic paradigm.

As we see dental practices and dentists all over the country, we see this polarization happening today. There are about 1% of the dental practices that see and adapt to the changes around them and economically grow, prosper and become wealthy in dentistry. The remaining 99% of the dental practices are flat, declining or are only having minor increases in their revenue.

The exciting thing is that you can choose which group you want to be in. Do you want to be in the 1% or the 99%? It is simply a choice. Remember, you just need to decide what you want and align yourself with the people that can help get you there. You can't do it on your own. If you could have done it on your own, you already would have.

There are some good consultants and coaches in the dental industry that can help you become more prosperous. I have used several over the years – some good and some "not so good". You want to, of course, stay away from the "not so good" ones.

You can build a practice that is recession proof. I believe that one of the best places to invest your money today is in the growth of your business. This is the place you are probably going to realize your greatest return on investment, in this economy. If you are grossing $80,000 a month and you invest in a dental consultant and double that to $160,000 per month, then you have a return on investment that beats anything in the stock market. This is also not just a one-time return, but one that continues on month after month. You can see the consultant's fee is a great investment.

Chapter Ten

Exit Strategy

How are you going to retire from practice one day?

It is very important to have a plan so your exit can be smooth and profitable. I find that most dentists don't have a clearly defined plan for exit strategy from their practice. If you don't have a plan for success, then you can usually plan to fail.

There are several different exit strategies for dental practices. I am going to share with you the plan I have implemented, which I believe works the best for the multi-million-dollar practices.

When should you start making an exit strategy?

**I believe you should start planning
your exit strategy at the same
time you are planning your
practice growth strategy.**

The reason for this is that your exit strategy is part of your practice growth strategy.

As many dentists get closer to retirement age, they start working less days and hours, therefore their production numbers go down.

**In other words, one of their largest
assets, their practice, is declining
in value at a time when they are
getting close to selling the practice.**

This makes no sense in the business world. In the normal business world, a company is intentionally grown to sell at the top of its productivity. The company is not intentionally slowed down and sold at a low point in its productivity. Unfortunately, this is what many dentists do because they have no exit strategy.

Some owner dentists hire an associate with the intention of selling the practice to that associate. The thought is that the owner doctor will slow down to the point he is ready to retire, and then sell the practice to the associate. This helps keep the numbers up as the owner doctor works less hours and therefore sees less patients.

The problem with this approach is now that the owner doctor has slowed down, much of the production numbers are being produced by the associate.

Since the practice is not in a large growth phase and the number of new patients is staying about the same, the owner doctor is really just transferring dentistry to the associate which he would normally have done prior to his cutting back on the number of hours he is working.

In my opinion, this plan to sell the practice to the associate is flawed, because the effective sales price of the practice is going down, since the associate is doing a growing percentage of the total production.

This associate is not going to want to pay full appraised value of the practice since a large part of the practice's value is a direct result of his efforts.

This often leads to disagreements because the intentions were not clearly defined at the start of the relationship. The associate often leaves because he can start his own practice for less than he can buy this practice at its appraised value, since a large portion of that value came from his "sweat equity".

When this associate leaves, he often takes with him a large portion of the patients, especially if there is no covenant-not-to-compete clause in the contract.

The owner dentist now has no buyer and has also possibly lost a substantial portion of his patients.

In this scenario, his practice is worth substantially less than it was a few years ago.

Practices typically sell for 60% of yearly gross collections if the practice has around a 40% profit margin. So, in the above scenario the owner doctor is only going to be able to sell his practice for around half of his declining collections.

Another exit strategy many doctors use is to hire an associate, sell the practice to that associate, and then the original owner doctor becomes an associate of this new owner.

Often, the original doctor will finance the practice for the purchasing doctor, which allows the original doctor to get his equity in the practice out over time plus interest.

This scenario works best if the practice is sold before the original doctor starts slowing down, and therefore keeps the sales price higher.

This type of arrangement works well for smaller practices where the purchase price is low enough for a single dentist to financially be able to afford the purchase price.

This book is about developing a multi-milliondollar practice. In this situation, there usually has to be a different exit strategy to allow the owner doctor to sell the practice for its appraised value.

This exit strategy allows the owner to sell his practice in increments to the different associates as it grows.

This strategy works well for a growing multimillion-dollar practice. This exit strategy will actually allow you to slow down as you get older, without hurting the value of your practice. The key to this strategy is growth over time, and selling percentages of the practice to multiple doctors as it grows. This is why you need to start putting this plan into place early in your process of building a multi-million-dollar practice.

Another advantage of this strategy is that it allows you to sell a large

practice in increments, over time.

Large practices are typically very difficult to sell. Banks are reluctant to loan millions of dollars to one dentist to purchase a large practice. With strategy you can also sell your practice in increments for 100% of collections.

Most dentists don't have the financial ability to purchase a multi-million-dollar practice, and most dentists also don't have the ability and/ or knowledge to manage a multi-million-dollar practice. Therefore, we must have a different exit strategy for the large growing multi-million-dollar practice.

This exit strategy requires that the practice continue growing. The time to hire an associate is when the practice grows to the point where the owner dentist cannot handle the load of new patients by himself.

**I find that many dentists hire
an associate too soon.**

When you hire an associate, you need to be very close to the point where you are not able to do all the dentistry that needs to be done. In other words, your practice is getting close to the place where <u>you</u> are the capacity blockage and patients have to be scheduled out too far into the future, because your schedule is so full.

If you have to schedule patients out two weeks or more to find a 90 minute appointment slot, then you have a capacity problem.

This capacity problem can be caused by other things that need to be fixed first before getting an associate. For instance, your schedule capacity problem may be from not enough treatment rooms, or staff, or there are time efficiency problems causing your procedures to take longer than they need to.

If you hire an associate before your practice is busy enough, then you are going to be giving him patients that you really have the time to see yourself.

You are just giving him patients in an effort to keep him busy. Therefore, as his production goes up, yours goes down.

I don't believe you need to add an associate until you have a plan to increase the number of new patients, so that your production doesn't suffer. There is no use in giving the new associate the dentistry that you have the time to do, and at the same time paying him to do that dentistry.

With our exit strategy, you hire an associate when the practice has the capacity to afford that associate by providing him with a sufficient number of new patients.

This associate is hired with the intention that he will buy a percentage of the practice in one year or so, if the relationship works out.

This gives you a 12 month "dating period" so you can both determine if this relationship should progress into a "marriage", which is the partnership buy-in.

I believe that associates need to have a partnership potential or many of them will just learn all they can from you and move on to open their own practice.

Having a pre-determined partnership buy-in contract is a win-win situation for both the owner and the associate.

The associate gets to own a part of a profitable growing practice without the risk of starting or purchasing a practice on his own. He also gets to learn the ins and outs of how to manage and build a multi-million-dollar practice. Since the practice is growing and has plans for continued growth, his percentage of ownership also grows in value.

The buy-in partnership price, which will take place one year later, is pre-determined in the contract when the associate is hired initially. This makes sure that there are no surprises or misunderstandings later on.

Each party knows exactly what the value of the practice is and about what the sales price is going to be in the future.

In a very large practice, the percentage buy-in is typically 25%, due to the high value of the practice. This price is basically 25% of the appraised practice value at the time the associate is hired, plus 50% of the increase in the value of the practice which took place during that 12 month period of time he worked as an associate.

There are triggered buy-in points for the associate after that first year. These points are based upon his production as a percentage of the owner doctor's production. These triggered buy-in points allow him to buy into the practice at 5% increments, until he has purchased the whole 25%. If he has already met those trigger buy-in point percentages after twelve months, then he can purchase all 25% at once if he chooses.

Now that the associate is a partner, he will be taking his share of the profits from the practice, which should more than cover his monthly note payments from the buy-in.

This approach allows you, as the owner dentist, to take equity out of your practice, over time. This can help with taxation and also allow you time to invest these proceeds to allow compounded growth before you retire.

This exit strategy also allows you to sell your practice in ever increasing increments, as your practice increases in value.

You will add partners and thus sell percentages, as the practice continues to grow. The last 25% that you sell will be to sell yourself out.

Another approach in a smaller, lower valued practice is to sell the associate 50% of the practice. As the practice grows and you add another partner, both you and your partner sell the new associate portions of your percentages until each partner owns 33.3%. If another partner is added, then each of the three partner's sell percentages of their ownership until each partner owns 25%.

As you can see, this is a great exit strategy that is a win-win for everyone. It also allows you to sell your practice for maximum value.

You need to start this plan early because it takes years to unfold and is a great strategy for the high growth multi-million-dollar practices.

The above explanation of this exit strategy is of course only hitting the high spots. There are lots of details I have left out. This is not something you can do on your own. You need a good attorney who has done these types of buyout contracts before. You also need a good dental coach/consultant to help you know when you are ready to make this type of move. If you start this exit strategy too soon, it can just turn into a huge cut in your income.

When this exit strategy is done properly, it is a huge win-win situation because everyone can get wealthy.

When you combine your million dollar net income over several years with an increasing incremental buyout over time, then this exit strategy really is the "icing on the cake" of your financial independence.

Chapter Eleven

The Power of Favor

I hope you make the decision to build a multi-million-dollar practice. I hope you make the commitment to spend the money and hire an experienced practice consultant and get a "do-whatever-it-takes mindset" to do this thing!

The reason I hope you do this is not just for the $1 million dollars you can make a year. Don't get me wrong, that is a pretty good motivation, but I don't think it is a strong enough motivation.

I don't believe that money alone
is a strong enough motivation
or a pure enough motivation.

Your passions and your dreams are stronger motivators which run deeper than money. I love the fact that I net more than $1 million a year out of my practice, but that is not what drives me to do it.

My dreams, my passions and my desire to make an impact on this world and other people by being successful are what drive me to keep pushing for the top.

I have found that most dentists that I meet are good people that care about others and really want to make a difference in the lives of their patients and their staff. Most dentists I know are involved in community, church and philanthropic endeavors.

You can't give from empty pockets. This is why I hope you "go for the gold" and build a multi-million-dollar practice.

You will be able to impact more lives in the world if you have deeper pockets from which to give. Being successful is so much more fun than just barely getting by financially.

There is another aspect of success that I want to touch on which has been a big part, and continues to be a big part of my quantum leap growth. This is in the area of favor.

I have found that the more money I give away, the more prosperous I become. This is a common theme in the lives of most wealthy people. They give out of their wealth and they get wealthier.

Just look at Bill Gates, Oprah Winfrey, Warren Buffet, etc. We are nowhere near their league in wealth and probably never will be, but they have a common thread of giving out of their wealth and they just keep getting wealthier and wealthier.

I suppose you could ask the questions...Do wealthy people give because they are wealthy? --or- Are they wealthy because they give? I believe it is largely because of the latter.

I have also found that the more I give, the more favor I have to be more successful.

The success becomes easier and easier the more I give away, and the more successful I am, the easier it becomes to give more because I have more.

I personally believe that this phenomenon is God's favor for success that He puts on our lives when we give. This is a biblical principle which has several scriptures that speak to this phenomenon of blessing and favor.

The important thing for you is to find those things that you are passionate about and let that ignite your dreams and your goals. Your financial success in dentistry has the ability to impact a lot of people in positive ways. Your wealth can help many people less fortunate than you are.

But, it is very hard to give if you are just barely getting by financially because your practice is not successful enough. With help, you can change that. You can't do it by yourself. If you could, you would have already done it.

You can't do it without some change in yourself because you are the one that got you to where you are now. It is going to require a different "you" to get you to where you want to go.

What got you here won't get you there.

You can make the necessary changes to become enormously successful! I did and I was messing up my success by doing the wrong things, just as much or more than the next guy.

What I want you to see is that your financial success is much bigger than you are. There are many other people in your life, like your family, your staff, your church, your synagogue, your favorite charity, etc., who are going to benefit from your making the commitment to do whatever it takes to build a multi-million-dollar practice.

Go for it! You can build a multi-million-dollar practice if you want to. Remember that if it has been done before, then it is probably possible for you too.

Dr. Mike Kesner

Chapter Twelve

Quantum Leap
Success In Dentistry

My consulting company – Quantum Leap Success In Dentistry – may be something that is right for you at this point in your career. We accept a limited number of clients every year who want to build a profitable multi-million-dollar practice. I'll be honest with you...it is a "high octane" 24 month program that is not for everyone.

To find out more about how we can work specifically with you and your practice, call the number on page 161 for a free one-hour phone consultation with one of our consultants. This is a $300 value that we extend to you for purchasing this book.

We will first fax you a form to provide us with some specific information about your practice. A consultant will call you at an appointed time to talk about your particular situation, and you can decide if Quantum Leap Success in Dentistry is right for you.

There are 3 different levels of membership available depending upon your situation and needs.

Platinum Plus Level: This level is designed for the doctor whose practice presently has an annual gross production amount of around $1 million per year or more, and who is highly committed to building his practice into a multi-million dollar practice.

Gold Level: This level is for the doctor whose present practice gross production is less than $1 million per year and/or is interested in a limited amount of growth in their practice at this point in their career. This program is also a good starting place for the doctor who is not yet ready for the Platinum Plus Level but plans to be in the near future.

Silver Level: This level is for the doctor who has limited resources and/or basic needs, but still has the desire for growth an improvements in their practice. This is a good entry level for the smaller practice.

Quantum Leap is a 24 month coaching and consulting program. Our goal and purpose are to develop a plan to help you build your practice into the practice of your dreams.

We start with a 2 day visit to your office from your personal dental consultant. The consultants that work for me have been in the dental consulting industry for many, many years. Like I said, there are good ones and not so good ones...I will not so humbly say that mine are the best.

This visit to your office will be a "top to bottom" analysis of your practice from which we will develop a 24 Month Master Plan to get you to the goals and aspirations that you have for your practice.

We will then go about implementing that master plan through doctor and staff training modules, with audio training of our systems, procedures and strategies, along with DVD training that actually show me and my team with real patients doing what we are teaching you to do.

There are periodic visits to your office by your personal coach. He will meet with you and your staff. He will train your staff in the various systems and strategies that we use, so that you can experience rapid increase in your success. You will also have two monthly scheduled phone calls with your coach.

We develop a marketing plan for your office with proven marketing pieces that bring in the new patients. We have free ad design and then printing and mailing of your direct mail marketing at our costs for Platinum Plus clients and discounted rates for Gold and Silver levels. This alone saves our clients thousands of dollars on their advertising. You get the huge advantage of using marketing pieces that have been proven to work in the most competitive markets. This saves you thousands of dollars by not having to do the "try it and see if it works" approach.

You will also have email access to your coach and to me.

Platinum Plus clients have two different scheduled one day visits to my office with their staff members to observe and ask questions as we see patients.

This allows you to see all the "moving parts" working together to make a multi-million-dollar practice. We then have dinner together where you and your staff can ask questions and get input and insights into your practice.

Most doctors and staff go home from these visits and have their best month ever. Their belief level goes up after "seeing it in action" and everything starts to come together where the office makes a huge jump. We frequently see offices increase 50% - 100% in their collections in a few months.

One office was stuck at around $80,000 a month and after they came to my office and spend a day, their very next month they produced $130,000. For the next several months they were doing $130,000 - $150,000 a month. They came for another visit to my office and their next month they produced $200,000. They are now doing $200,000 - $250,000 in production per month!

Seeing really is believing. In addition to belief, the doctor and the staff get to see all the parts working together which causes understanding to happen on a different level. The doctor and team then goes home and does it themselves.

Another service we provide is periodic recorded audit calls to your front desk to make sure they are properly handling the phone as they have been taught by your coach. You and the team member will receive a recording of the phone call and your coach will work with that staff member to get them up to speed if they "fail" the phone call.

Your consultant will monitor all of your practice's numbers and statistics. This allows your consultant to make sure that everything is staying on track and in line with your goals. They will be monitoring your schedule and making sure your staff is scheduling you for maximum profitability. He will also monitor all of your numbers and alert you of any imbalances and how to fix them before they become a very expensive problem. You will also receive daily, weekly and monthly reports of these vital statistics.

**For our Platinum Plus clients
this comes with a market area
exclusivity for their practices so we
won't consult any other dentist in
close proximity to their practice.**

If you want to find out more, you can visit our website. You can download an application form and fax it back to receive you free one-hour phone consultation.

You can also follow us on Facebook and Twitter to connect with our practice tips video blogs from Dr. Kesner.

I hope this book has been an inspiration for you to dream big things for your dental practice and for your life and future. You can accomplish your dreams and goals to build that multi-million-dollar dental practice and build the practice of your dreams!

Website: www.QLSuccess.com

Email: info@QLSuccess.com

            drkesner@QLSuccess.com

Phone: 480-282-8989

Fax: 480-899-1587

Chapter Thirteen

What Our Clients Are Saying

"After I and some of my staff spent a day at Dr. Kesner's office, I was amazed at how much dentistry he and his staff could do in a day. They made it look so easy. I immediately went home and implemented several of the things we learned after watching and talking to Dr. Kesner. We went from doing around a $100,000 per month to $180,000 the next month."

Dr. Mark D.

Tulsa, OK

"Since becoming a client of Quantum Leap, I have seen an improvement in virtually every statistic - new patients, patient volume, billing and collections. The most significant improvement in my practice however is not something that statistics show. That is the area of stress. Stress has been reduced greatly and that makes practice a whole lot easier and more fun too. This stress reduction is the result of the efficient and effective management systems which we have implemented with your guidance."

Dr. Mike B.

Seattle, WA

"I've been in practice for over 25 years and have worked with many nationally known dental consultants. I look for someone who has experience, wisdom, integrity and the ability to make things happen. I found all of these with Quantum Leap and more. They have helped us grow the practice even in tough economic times. I can't recommend them more highly."

Dr. Guy N.

Temecula, CA

"Quantum Leap came to our practice at a time our practice needed staff guidance. The rapport with our team was super and the open door policy was what we needed.

Their handling of some difficult decisions involving the team was inspirational."

Dr. Sam C.

St. Louis, MO

"I have been in practice for many years and have used many different consulting companies. Quantum Leap is the only one that got me a quick and substantial increase in my production and collections. My numbers were up over 20% after only 2 months with Quantum Leap. I have always produced a lot in my practice but never kept very much. Now I have money left over after everything gets paid."

Dr. Avis B.

Southfield, MI

"I have been in practice for only 2 years. Quantum Leap has moved my collections up to $170,000 per month in only 6 months! My staff loves coming to work because they get to run the practice and get my patients to do the dentistry they need. They also get some great monthly bonuses. With Dr. Kesner as my role model my practice is going to continue to grow by leaps and bounds."

Dr. Thinh H.

Olympia, WA

"Quantum Leap has a business model that has allowed me to increase my revenue by 15% in the last 4 months when all the other dentists in my area are down by 15%. You don't have to be a victim of this economy. With what Dr. Kesner teaches I have a thriving practice that continues to grow each month even though the area I practice in is economically depressed."

Dr. George L.

Durango, CO

"Quantum Leap stepped right in and helped us tweak our marketing card campaign, and as a result, more new patients are being seen each month. They helped us implement new systems to improve effectiveness in new patient exams, case presentations, scheduling, financial arrangements, recall, collections, internal marketing and others. They helped in defining goals for the office, as well as clarify each staff member's duties, responsibilities and accountability. Even in this down economy, our office production and collections have steadily increased, something that I am positive would not have happened without their coaching. I am optimistic that we will continue to have increasing success as we continue to work with Quantum Leap."

Dr. Andy S.

Chandler, AZ

Free One-Hour Phone Consultation ($300 Value)

Call 480-282-8989 to set up a time to talk with one of our practice consultants. Mention that you have the free one-hour phone consultation offer from this book. You will be able to talk with the consultant about the specifics of your practice and see if Quantum Leap Success In Dentistry is right for you.

We reserve the right to stop this offer at any time. We also reserve the right to refuse services to any doctor or practice if we believe Quantum Leap Success In Dentistry is not a proper match for you. We also reserve the right to refuse services if we already have a client in your area.